Economic theory and policy for trading blocks

CHRISTOPHER BLISS

Economic theory and policy for trading blocks

Manchester University Press
Manchester and New York

distributed exclusively in the USA and Canada by St Martin's Press

Published by Manchester University Press
Oxford Road, Manchester M13 9NR, UK
and Room 400, 175 Fifth Avenue, New York, NY 10010, USA

Distributed exclusively in the USA and Canada
by St. Martin's Press, Inc., 175 Fifth Avenue, New York,
NY 10010, USA

British Library Cataloguing-in-Publication Data
A catalogue record is available from the British Library

Library of Congress Cataloguing-in-Publication Data

Bliss, C. J.
Economic theory and policy for trading blocks / Christopher Bliss.
p. cm.
"This volume grew out of the 1992 University of Manchester Economics Special Lectures ... delivered in March 1992, ... considerably expanded and elaborated"—Pref.
Includes bibliographical references.
ISBN 0-7190-4018-3 (cl)
1. Commercial policy. 2. Trading blocks. 3. Protectionism. 4. Foreign exchange. I. Title.
HF1411.B615 1994
338.9–dc20 93-50583

ISBN 0 7190 4018 3 *hardback*

Typeset in Great Britain
by P&R Typesetters Ltd, Salisbury, Wilts
Printed in Great Britain
by Bookcraft (Bath) Ltd

CONTENTS

To Ghada

PREFACE

This volume grew out of the 1992 University of Manchester Economics Department Special Lectures, which were delivered in March 1992, well over a year ago at the time of completing the manuscript for delivery to the publishers. This large passage of time is accounted for by the fact that in preparing the material for publication I have considerably expanded and elaborated the argument. There is a second reason as well. More than a year's worth of events has required of me substantial changes of emphasis. In the original text, for instance, I took the European Monetary System to be the leading example of a currency block. I looked critically at its function and at the claims made for it as an intra-block trade promoter, or as a low-inflation-rate coordinator. Yet I did not tell my audience, as with the benefit of hindsight I now know I should have done, that the wide EMS would shortly embark on a period of crisis, a process of uncontrollable dismemberment and eventual collapse.

The lesson must be that to apply the apparatus of theoretical and academic analysis to very current economic problems and institutions is always to run the risk that the course of history will turn particular arguments and positions into out-of-their-time curiosities. Yet the risk is worth running. It is good for economic theory to 'get its teeth into' current policy issues, good for students of economic theory to see how this may be attempted, and what problems are encountered when the attempt is made. Also, however much developments in institutions may make particular features of a case obsolete, there is always a core to a serious analysis of an important problem which will retain lasting value, and with this in mind I have tried to concentrate on considerations which are likely to hold their relevance through institutional changes. An outstanding example of the durability of the fundamental is provided by Viner's nearly forty-year-old analysis of trade creation and trade diversion in a customs union. For all the volumes of extensions and qualifications which have been addressed to Viner's argument, it continues to voice the most important single point to be made about the economic effects of a customs union – then, today, or in the future.

By the time this book goes to press, the world has changed still more. The Maastricht Treaty is ratified and the Uruguay round negotiations have concluded in a GATT deal which achieves many, though not all, the original objectives. I have made no attempt to update the discussion. That would involve far too many changes and would risk introducing new anomalies. So the text remains frozen in the time when it was written down. The reader will see this and does not need me to explain recent history.

It is embarrassing for an author to have to admit that he suffered uncertainty concerning how to spell the title of his book. Trading blocks are conglomerates of nations acting in unison and the word *Bloc*, which covers that meaning precisely, is very arguably correct. Yet economists have often adopted the spelling *block* and that is employed throughout the present volume. I apologise to those who dislike this usage but I am absolutely unwilling to enter into any correspondence on the issue.

It is impossible for a trade theorist to visit the Economics Department at Manchester without remembering that Harry Johnson and Arthur Lewis were professors there. These great economists both believed that economic theory could illuminate real life policy issues, and their work has surely outlived the particular circumstances from which it drew its original inspiration. If it is absurdly optimistic to hope that formal theory can throw light on our present problems for the reform and design of international economic institutions, then Manchester is the right place to indulge that optimism.

In preparing the lectures and developing them into a book, I have become indebted to many people. First, I thank the members of the Department of Economics at the University of Manchester, for inviting me to give the 1992 Special Lectures in Economics and for their excellent hospitality during my visit to Manchester. In addition, non-incriminating appreciation for encouragement, comments and information go to Jagdish Bhagwati, Heather Bliss, Alan Deardorff, James Forder, Vijay Joshi, Stan Metcalfe, Lynden Moore, Amelia Porges, Peter Sinclair, T. N. Srinivasan, Ian Steedman, John Vickers, David Vines and Alan Winters.

Oxford,
September 1993

INTRODUCTION

The idea that the world is breaking up into trade blocks is popular. It is frequently invoked in press articles and in television programmes. Academics discuss it and the World Bank has organised at least one conference on the subject.[1] Yet even the definition of a trade block is, as I shall argue, problematic. Also, the view of what trade blocks entail, and whether they represent a good or a bad development, that is implicit in some discussions, is superficial. Looseness of the definition of a trade block is in turn reflected in different views of how important is the tendency towards block formation. The answer to the empirical question of how strong is the trend towards trade block formation obviously depends upon the definition of a trade block, and questions of definition and of the empirical prevalence of blocks are among the questions considered in Chapter 1.

One of the duties of academics and commentators is to document what is happening in the world regardless of whether anything can be done to affect these developments. Yet it is even more interesting when comment and analysis can contribute to a debate about the formation of real policy. In this connection it is fortunate that the formation of world trade policy is in an active phase at the present time, even if the process is burdened with many problems, both technical and political. The General Agreement on Tariffs and Trade (the GATT), one of the great building blocks of the post-war world order, is being reformed and revised – at least the intention of leading powers is that this should happen. Some of the pressures for the reform of the GATT come from trade blocks, or from the fear of them, but the main reason why the reform of the GATT is on the agenda is that the GATT is old and has become decreasingly relevant to the practices of trade and trade management in today's world.

GATT reform and trade block issues are not the same, but they interconnect in two ways. First, rules for blocks and for inter-block trade are one of the areas that an ideal reformed GATT should address, as the original GATT did, though inadequately, as I shall explain. Secondly, in so far as there are blocks, and there is one at least in the shape of the European Communities (the EC), or just large trade nations, such as Japan, these are leading negotiators in the GATT reform discussions, and without their agreement there will be no successful reform. For this reason it makes sense to discuss the reform of international trade along with trade blocks. Chapter 2 discusses the sources of protectionist pressures, the history of the GATT, the nature of its problems, and the agenda for a new treaty for the regulation of international trade law.

As well as looking at practical issues, this volume is concerned with economic theory. What effects trade blocks will have, and how they should be designed, are questions for theory, and one of my objectives is to investigate how far existing economic theory can throw light on trade blocks and their effects on trade and welfare. There is a great deal of economic theory that can be applied to this issue, chief among it the rich literature on customs union theory. This literature is reconsidered for application to the contemporary context. Not much that is fundamentally new had to be done for this purpose, because the essential results are already there, although possibly the most important result is not as well known as it deserves to be. Where new work had to be done is in the development of the connections between customs union theory and taxation theory further than is usually done. The main theoretical techniques and conclusions are developed and explained in Chapter 3.

The lesson to which the theory points is that there is not a single entity called a trade block, but rather that a trade block can be designed to more than one specification. This is obvious where commercial relations with the outside world are concerned. They must be harmonised to some extent at least, and plainly they can take more than one specific form. In addition, the internal organisation of a block, which includes such matters as taxation and its harmonisation, or non-harmonisation, subsidy provision and competition regulation, and restrictions (or their absence) on the mobility of labour and capital within the block, are all variables that importantly affect how a block operates and how its formation will influence welfare inside and outside the block.

Two particular issues within the broad framework sketched above receive detailed attention in Chapters 4 and 5. These are, first, the use of compensatory transfer schemes to redistribute between various groups or interests within the block, either as a consequence of more free trade within the block, or, more broadly, to alleviate their relative deprivation in an income comparison with others inside the block. The EC envisaged the use of such schemes from its foundation in the original community of six members and has developed their funding and employment extensively. Yet the ideas behind these schemes have sometimes seemed simplistic and it will be argued that their application deserves a more rigorous and critical evaluation than it has so far received.

Whatever criticism of particular transfer schemes may be advanced, transfer and compensation in one form or another seem to be essential concepts for understanding block formation and block function. This is not just because the root economic theory that shows that a block can be generally welfare improving requires the use of compensatory transfers, although that is importantly the case. Trade with countries outside the block can be used, and should be used, as a substitute for external aid. Chapter 4 discusses all these issues in as much depth as space allows.

Compensation, whether in the form of direct transfer, or in the form of market access, affects, and can substitute for, factor migration, particularly the migration of labour within the block and from outside the block. This type of consideration was certainly influential in the idea of extending the USA–Canada free trade agreement to take in Mexico, giving birth to the concept of a North-American Free Trade Area (NAFTA). That letting in Mexican products within a NAFTA might be a substitute for a greater and a hard-to-control inflow of Mexican migrants into the USA was noted quite explicitly by many commentators on the proposal. Chapter 5 examines several issues posed by the existence of migration, starting from a discussion of how, if at all, migration questions differ from other resource allocation issues in a general equilibrium.

As is well known, international economic theory has undergone a metamorphic transformation during the last decade. The old perfect competition models that dominated the literature for so long now have to share the stage with new international economic theory models based on increasing returns to scale in production and game-theory-modelled interactions between large producers and policy makers. It would be interesting in any case to see how block formation is affected by imperfect competition, and, in addition, to investigate how a reformed trade regime might legislate for concentrations of economic power and their effects. The exercise, however, is not merely academic. Real policy makers have already noticed the importance of monopoly and competition control. The EC, for instance, regulates competition centrally and internationally, and has played with the idea of strategic trade promotion. To see how this area is affected by block formation, some new theory has had to be developed, although it is theory that grows easily and naturally out of existing work. These results and a wider-ranging discussion of the implications of increasing returns and large producers for trade blocks are included in Chapter 6.

The idea that the world is breaking up into trade blocks was mentioned without saying what precisely defines a trade block. Central to the concept must be a greater freedom of internal trade for block members with the necessary implications for the joint conduct of external economic relations, including a common external tariff or internal protocols for customs officers, as appropriate. As these are minimum requirements, it follows that many additional features may, or may not, be added as optional extras. For instance, there may or may not be free mobility of factors within the block. The NAFTA does not propose this where labour is concerned; the EC has it in principle, but less in practice.

Similarly, trade block members may not use the same currency for internal transactions but if they do not they may stabilise their exchange rates, either wholly or, more easily, partially. The relationship between a currency block and a trade block is examined in Chapter 7. The European Monetary System (EMS) and the currency union (EMU) promoted by the Maastricht Treaty[2] are leading examples of exchange rate stabilisation within a block. The volume of writing that currency union and the EMS have generated in recent years is enormous. I make no attempt to survey it or to reflect all its ideas in this last analytical chapter. Instead I offer a somewhat different perspective from the usual one, concentrating on the real resource allocation effects of exchange rate stabilisation.

It is clear that the economic theory and policy issues posed by the trade block and by allied issues in trade rule reform are potentially vast, and it will be seen that this book is small, although it is considerably longer than the lectures out of which it developed. It follows that the reader is offered only a short tour of an area that would repay much more lengthy study. What I have tried to achieve is more limited. I hope that the analysis and arguments that follow will convince my readers that the trade block is not simply a political–economic tangle not amenable to economic analysis, but that the apparatus of rigorous theory can throw much light on its design. A similar case can be made for viewing GATT reform from a theoretical perspective.

The concluding Chapter 8 argues that, while one may need an optimistic temperament to believe that the conduct of world trade will move somewhat away from damaging restrictions answering narrow interests, it is not absurd to hope that this may happen. The benefits of liberal trade are huge; the tendencies towards block formation themselves reflect the recognition of that fact. Most governments would like to take the benefits of liberal trade while escaping from the awkward political difficulties that free trade can generate for the individual government at particular times. But these governments know that it is not a real possibility for each individual party to free-ride. So they want there to be rules, although they will of course manoeuvre to establish rules favourable to their particular situations. Then there has to be compromise and a giving and taking. Good institutional design, however, pushes the utility possibility frontier outwards, and that can only smooth the process of negotiating the difficult agreements and compromises required.

Although a great deal of my argument will be accessible to any reader who has studied introductory international trade theory, there are some unavoidably technical arguments. I have tried to make the ideas behind these arguments as accessible as possible, without obscuring the fact that technical considerations are involved. In expositing some theoretical ideas a compromise has to be struck between the needs of the less mathematically fluent reader and the reader who prefers a mathematical treatment. For this reason some of the more technical and mathematical arguments are put into appendices at the end of the relevant chapter. In the case of Chapter 6, where a large part of the underlying argument consists of the working of mathematical examples, this produces the odd result that the appendix is slightly longer than the main body of the chapter. I have taken care, however, to lay out the intuitive basis of the results in the non-technical part of the chapter. Hence the reader not inclined to do so will be able to follow the argument without working through the appendix.

Notes

1 See de Melo and Panagariya (1993).

2 In common with popular usage, I always refer to the Maastricht Treaty, rather than using the more formally correct term Treaty on European Union.

CHAPTER 1

Trade blocks

1.1 What is a trade block?

According to a widely disseminated view, the world is breaking up into trade blocks. This description is often advanced as a trend that exists and that we had better react to, because it is going to happen anyway. Some commentators think the trend unfortunate, others seem to welcome it, but rarely is the existence of the trend questioned. Many of those who believe that it is happening also believe that it is practically unavoidable. In fact the evidence in favour of widespread block formation among the world's trading nations is not as impressive as many accounts would lead one to expect. To decide the question we need to determine what a trade block is, and that exercise is far from trivial. The weakest definition would say that a trade block consists of a group of countries that trade intensely with each other. That definition is unsatisfactory by itself, because intense trade could reflect no more than differences in comparative advantage. So to talk of a trade block we must require that policy arrangements have somehow brought it about that trade flows more easily and considerably between a particular group of countries than between other groups of countries enjoying similar differences in comparative advantage. An obvious case of policy having that effect would be the free trade area, the customs union or the single market.

For the purpose of many of the arguments developed in this volume, the particular distinctions between free trade area, customs union or single market are not of great significance. What mainly matters is that each of these arrangements allows trade between the participating countries to take place more easily and at lower cost. Yet it is important to be clear at least about what the distinctions entail. The proposed North-American Free Trade Area (NAFTA), which is a free trade area, the European Community (EC), which was a customs union from its inception, and the new single-market EC, which was supposed to start life on 1 January 1993, will serve as examples. With a free trade area, internal trade must be free of tariffs or other restrictions, but external tariffs can be levied and can differ between countries. Thus, in the case of the NAFTA, the tariff charged by Canada on the import of office equipment from Germany need not equal the tariff charged by Mexico on the same import. For this reason, a free trade area requires internal customs posts and certificates of origin for goods moving within the area. To establish a free trade area is in principle relatively easy from the administrative point of view for just this reason. Existing customs officials have to be given a new schedule of tariff rates, including zero rates for goods originating inside the free trade area, and told to go on doing just what they were doing before.

In fact things are never as simple as that account would suggest. The problems arise because of the potential complexities that hide behind the simple idea that some goods originate inside the free trade area, and some by implication outside. Things would be that simple if all output were produced by fully vertically integrated production processes, producing finished outputs from domestic factors of production, or if bought-in inputs were always purchased from similar domestic producers. In reality, however, many production processes are value added processes that make use of manufactured inputs to produce more processed products of higher value. An obvious example would be the use of steel, produced by a steel maker, to manufacture motor vehicles in a separate factory. To illustrate the problems that can arise, consider the simplest possible free trade area consisting of just two countries, Country A and Country B. Suppose that aluminium ladders can either be imported from outside the free trade area or be manufactured from aluminium in a form suitable for melting and moulding. For some reason, Country A has a high tariff on aluminium ladders, while Country B has a low tariff on the same product. The reason might be that Country B has no capacity to protect, and we should assume for the sake of this example that it imports ladders to meet its own demand from the outside world.

Now the free trade area is formed but the countries keep their existing external tariffs. So far as the ladder sector is concerned, the free trade area has no effect. Ladders are cheap in Country B, as they have always been, and expensive in Country A. An attempt to export them from B to A to make a profit is of no avail, however. The customs officials note that the ladders were manufactured outside the free trade area and charge A's high external tariff.

Perhaps the reason why Country B had no aluminium ladders capacity is that it had no aluminium smelting capacity. In that case it made sense to import finished ladders. With the free trade area there is a new incentive to import aluminium to make into Country B manufactured ladders to export to Country A. As the outside world is more efficient at producing finished ladders than is Country B, this is a movement away from world production efficiency. The issue of how trade block arrangements affect efficiency will be explored in Chapter 3. In any case, the free trade area regulations are most unlikely to allow into a member country free of duty any product finished in another member country without regard to its foreign content. The rules might say, for instance, that, as half the value of a Country B ladder is Country B value added and half is raw aluminium, the ladder must pay half Country A's external duty on aluminium

It is useful to have a name for the problem of designing and administering rules for trade within a free trade area. It will be called the certificate of origin problem. If Country B is no better at turning aluminium into ladders than any other country and has no aluminium smelting capacity, a certificate of origin rule such as the one described above would defeat the tariff-hopping scheme of manufacturing ladders in B. The example is unrealistic in the following respect. Individual countries rarely charge significant tariffs on raw material imports but do charge tariffs on products made from the same raw materials. This high effective protection of the value added activities greatly disadvantages the same value added activity in outside countries.

The simple example could be elaborated. Obviously the administration of customs posts could be made impossibly complicated if a mad logic of dissecting goods into their within-the-free-trade-area and out-of-area value components were taken too far, and in practice simple rules of thumb are applied, which can in turn give rise to anomalies. On the other hand, a completely slack administration of rules of origin would defeat the purpose of the external tariffs of area member countries, which is, presumably, to protect domestic value added activities. If Country A has a high tariff to protect an activity that otherwise would be unable to compete with the outside world, it is not going to be happy to see a so-called 'hammer and screwdriver' factory set up in its partner Country B to feed outside production into its markets. The disparaging description 'hammer and screwdriver' is intended to convey the idea that a certain plant is not a genuine manufacturer, but is simply breaking open cases of imported components and assembling them.

The administration of within-area trade for a free trade area with certificates of origin or similar rules will be more difficult:

- the more member countries have very different external tariffs;
- the more member countries have strongly divergent comparative advantages and trade structures; and
- the greater is the extent of the protection provided by the external tariffs of the free trade area.

The difficulties associated with member countries having very different external tariff rates are resolved if the member nations of a free trade group adopt a common external tariff, which means that they all charge the same tariff rates on imports from the outside world. With the same regulations in operation at all points of entry to the union, there is in principle no need for customs officers at internal borders to collect tariffs on the movement of commodities originating outside the union. With free trade inside the union, internal customs barriers should become redundant. This is called a customs union.

The EC has a common external tariff, which means that the tariff charged by Belgium on the import of office equipment from the United States must be the same as the tariff charged by Italy on the same import, both being equal to the EC's common external tariff for office equipment. Yet years after its foundation, the EC had failed to abolish internal customs barriers, and their presence continued to have more than trivial effects, with trucks typically spending up to 24 hours to clear customs at the Italian border. That reminds us that true customs unification is not easy to achieve. The problem was not that the EC failed to establish a Community-wide centrally controlled customs administration, comparable to US customs. It seems that national port of entry customs officials in the EC did very much what US customs officials do.

Rather the difficulties arose because the abolition of internal barriers to trade in a free trade union, regardless of its particular character, is very difficult to achieve. It is straightforward to prohibit the collection of tariffs, or the operation of quotas, at internal borders. Yet this leaves numerous possible, and often actual, barriers in place, all of which may require the intervention of customs officials to police them. They include quotas on imports from a source external to the union imposed by a particular member nation, which can obviously be regulated only by national border officials; national standards rules; health and safety regulations, and more besides.

There are also complications for trade that arise from the fact that separate national administrations are involved. As an illustration, consider that, because value added tax (VAT) rates differ between EC member states, the revenue authorities in the different countries have to monitor trade to collect extra VAT where the rate is lower in the source country, or remit it where the rate in the source country is higher. After January 1993 this paperwork does not take place at customs posts at national frontiers but is transferred to transactions between businesses and revenue authorities inside borders. The single market will differ significantly from the national market of one sovereign nation.

The United States of America comes close to being the perfect single market. It is the case that formal barriers to trade within the USA are illegal. It has one national customs administration, and no state-to-state border customs posts. It does, however, have widely varying state laws and regulations, which somewhat inconvenience the completely free flow of goods and services between different states. Moreover it does not have uniform sales taxes and this has sometimes caused diversion of trade across state boundaries and consequent discontent from affected sellers.

The ideal single market would not suffer from any barriers to trade arising from areas with conflicting legal regimes, or any comparable non-tariff, non-customs-post regulated, restriction. To implement such an arrangement is an extremely ambitious enterprise to undertake. Indeed the European single market initiative is perhaps the only example in history in which this has been attempted short of full political union. And full political union of independent nations, it is worth recalling, has mostly in the past been imposed, more or less, in the aftermath of war. The newly independent states of ex-colonial North America did merge their sovereignty voluntarily. Yet their freedom was purchased by war, and the context in which they opted for federation was one in which their collective defence remained a major consideration. Even in that context, their surrender of their sovereignty was about as partial as they could make it in the circumstances.

The single market in the European model does more than permit the free movement of goods and services. It also allows in principle for the uninhibited movement of factors, particularly capital and labour. Again a simple idea is complicated when translated into practice. It is easiest with capital because, in a sense, capital switches nationality automatically when it migrates. Suppose, for instance, that shareholders in one member country enjoy different rights of disclosure than those enjoyed by another, and that the single market legislation does not impose common rules. Then capital migrating from one country to another in effect surrenders its national rights and takes on those of the destination country.

Labour, however, is different from capital in that it cannot be as anonymous, at least not in its skilled or professionally qualified form. For skilled labour to be able to migrate, mutual recognition of qualifications is required, and this was in principle established by the single European market treaty. In practice, the processes whereby professional establishment is affected are complex and extremely variable. This is partly because national traditions diverge, and partly because the professions everywhere play the role of regulating entry on the craft union model.

Migrant labour, like capital, could surrender its national employment rights at the border to take on the rights given by the destination nation and this was allowed in the design of the European single market. The authors of the Maastricht Treaty, however, attempted to constrain the extent to which conditions of employment could vary in the different member states by means of the Social Chapter. The chapter, however, addresses only certain specific matters, leaving others outside the legislative framework. In the event, Britain reserved for itself an opt-out from the Social Chapter, so that even its partial implications for employment conditions will not become Community-wide even if the Maastricht Treaty is eventually ratified by all member states. The question of how far uniformity of factor employment conditions should be a required feature of a trade block is examined as an issue of economic theory in Chapter 5.

Now that free trade arrangements between nations in their various forms have been noted, these distinctions will be set aside for the most part in what follows. This avoids tediously repetitive reference to the different cases even when the differences are not relevant to the point at hand. A trading union is a useful general term, with the free trade area, the customs union and the single market all being particular cases of the trading union. The avoidance of the term 'trade block' at this stage is deliberate. What a trade block is and how important its role may be in the contemporary international economy is an issue still to be resolved.

A trading union should trade extensively with itself; that is what it is for. In what sense does that make a trading union a trade block? Consider another aspect of the trade block. The countries of a trade block should coordinate their trade relations with the outside world. They may, for instance, confer over their administration of their external tariffs. They must certainly do that if they set a common external tariff, but they could participate collectively in tariff-fixing negotiations without necessarily sharing a common external tariff. An example of how this might happen is provided by the Cairns group of food-exporting countries, which exists only as a trade negotiating group. The example of the Cairns group demonstrates well the distinction between a trade block and the distinct notion of an interest group of trading nations, formed for the purpose of more effectively representing shared interests in international trade reform negotiations. Indeed in many ways the two cases are directly opposed. A trade block is usually assumed to want to promote trade among its own members, at the expense of trade with the outside world on a pessimistic view. In so far as the Cairns group is typical, the trade interest group is more concerned with promoting the trade of its members with the rest of the world, or in protecting trade with the rest of the world against trade-diverting interventions by trade blocks.

If that is the difference between the trade block and the trade interest group, both share another feature in common. They are coalitions of nations, and although they may seem to form policy or to negotiate as a single body, they always unite interests that diverge to some extent. The trade interest group is likely to be more united where interests and outcome weightings are concerned than the trade block. The reason is that closely shared interests almost define the composition of a trade interest group.

Because it must constitute a voluntary association of sovereign nations, it might seem that shared interests should also be an essential feature of trade block members. Yet this is true only in a fairly trivial sense. First, political objectives often drive economic block formation, as was notably the case with the EC, and shared political objectives can coexist with very different economic interests. Secondly, a leading motive for joining a trading union may be fear of exclusion from the trade benefits of membership, the existence of which fear does not imply a complete harmony of interest with other members of the union. Lastly, a union may offer, for whatever reason, what are in effect financial inducements to expand its membership in the form of transfers or subsidies.

The EC offers inducements to poorer countries to join, through its structural funds, cohesion funding and similar arrangements. These schemes are the vehicles of the the equalisation written into the original

Treaty of Rome and intended to mitigate inequalities of economic development within the community of six.[1] They were not designed to provide inducements for non-members to join. The relevant articles of the treaty have been little amended, although their application has been extended, partly in response to the growing diversity of the union. With the principle of compensatory funding in place, it would have provided an inducement to poorer countries to join even if that funding had not been extended. Why did the core EC accept poor and potentially burdensome new members? Again the motives were mainly political, membership, for instance, serving as an inducement to the maintenance of democracy in countries where this outcome was felt to be uncertain.

Such considerations help to explain why it has proved difficult to form a trade interest group to represent the interests of the developing countries in the Uruguay Round negotiations with anything like the effectiveness of the Cairns group. The developing countries lack any of the essential ingredients for the successful formation of either a trade block or a trade interest group. For trade block formation they are without the impetus of shared political objectives – often in practice those of a leading nation or small group of nations. Even neglecting the leading role of politics, large gains, or what can be represented as large gains, from increased trade within the group are seldom present. For the developing countries the conditions for trade interest group formation might seem closer to realisation, but this is true only if the objectives of the interest group are defined in general and rather unfocused terms. Obviously, rampant protectionism by industrial countries is against the interests of nearly all developing countries. Yet, as soon as one gets down to detail, developing country interests start to diverge. We could not assume, for instance, that all developing countries would oppose the use of certain mechanisms of trade intervention that are frequently deployed against them, such as the anti-dumping tariff or quota. Quotas can protect the position of an existing developing country exporter from competition from other developing country producers, thus forming an interest against their prohibition.

More generally, the great variability of the economic situations of the developing countries mitigates against their forming a united front. With simple tests, notice that many developing countries are food importers but some are food exporters; many developing countries are energy importers but some are energy exporters; some developing countries have rapidly growing manufactures exports, others hardly at all; and so on. This might suggest that sub-sets of developing countries could be better placed to form like-interested coalitions, and that is correct, but the conditions for successful interest coalition formation are not easy to meet. For countries to work together effectively, and this is not a point that applies only to developing countries, more than a unity of interest is required. Cultural, political or historical closeness play an important part in enabling the group to work harmoniously together. Yet these natural accords may well run in different directions from those that define accord of interest from the economic point of view.

1.2 The trade block as a currency union

So far the trading union has been considered exclusively from the point of view of real trade, real comparative advantage, and taking into account the way in which such real interventions as cuts in within-union tariffs may promote trade between union members. On a quite different interpretation, a trade block is a currency block. That could mean, at the strongest, a group of nations that all use the same currency in trade, or, on a weaker interpretation, a group of nations that coordinate their policies so as to stabilise their nominal exchange rates. In either case a currency block is very differently constituted than a trade block, and it does not necessarily allow free movement of goods, or even of capital, between its member countries. In a sense the economic world that Bretton Woods created was a nearly world-wide dollar block. Yet severe capital movement restrictions, and significant trade restrictions regulated by the GATT, were a feature of those arrangements. The question of what currency alignment does and does not do will be examined in detail in Chapter 7. Yet regardless of what economic analysis may conclude, currency block weight is widely taken to stand for economic power. Part of the pressure for European currency union springs from a wish to see a European currency stand beside the dollar, or the yen, as an equal partner, in a way that, this case would imply, it cannot do while Europe trades in numerous separate currencies, even if their exchange rates are coordinated. It seems that the idea of a trade block is far from clear cut. A trade block may be a large country, a currency area, a customs union, some other variety of trading union, any combination of these, or something else besides. Yet coordination of policy, whether with regard to trade or to exchange rates, is at the heart of the idea. To take the discussion further we need to examine the current situation in detail.

1.3 The current situation

At present we have one trade block at least in the form of a customs union, partly achieved single market and putative currency area in the EC.[2]. An old free trade area, EFTA, will mainly merge with the EC. A recently planned free trade area, NAFTA, will unite the economies of the USA, Canada and Mexico if it comes into effect. The Cairns group of food-exporting countries exists only as a trade negotiating group. And there is Japan. On the time-honoured principle, make the facts fit your model, Japan should be a trade block. In order to see Japan as a trade block, one has to find evidence that a yen block, led by Japan, is forming in East Asia and the Pacific, its nations condensing into a trade-regulating, Japanese-investment-coordinated, common currency block. In fact, where trade is concerned, the evidence for this case is not compelling. This nicely illustrates the point that whether or not a particular case is a trade block depends on the definition of a trade block.

Cross-investment (mainly from Japan) has grown more rapidly than intra-block trade, and the influence of the yen has undoubtedly grown. That this amounts to much less than the creation of an East Asian trade block is argued in detail by Jeffrey Frankel in his wide-ranging and impressive American Express Bank prize-winning essay.[3] Even where it can be shown that Japan is working to promote trade with South East Asian countries, this may be weak evidence of its block-promoting tastes. Japanese planners have to take into account the difficulties that Japan has already experienced in trading with the industrial countries of the North – the quotas, voluntary export restraints and anti-dumping moves – and consider the possibility that such restraints on trade will grow and widen their reach. It would be imprudent of Japan not to look to alternative trading areas where similar problems may be less likely to arise. In short, a trade block in one part of the world, or several, may encourage the formation of blocks elsewhere. For many purposes it makes little difference where the emphasis is placed or exactly how the evidence regarding trade block formation is interpreted. Even if Japan acts entirely alone, it is a big player in world trade and investment. That it is a sovereign nation state should mean in principle that it exercises rational and coordinated policy with regard to its exchange rate and with regard to policy affecting trade with the rest of the world.

In fact nations, like trade areas, consist of consortiums of interests, defined by factors of production (general and specific), consumption groups, regions and non-economic interests. Hence for any nation interest conflict is characteristic of policy formation. Sometimes these difficulties are more acute where the large nation is concerned, but the opposite outcome is not improbable. Small countries indeed provide the most acute examples of political tension in the world. Large Japan has its small, usually part-time, farmers, who represent a powerful and effective lobby for agricultural protection, despite the fact that the share of agricultural production in Japanese national product is less than 2%. Without the energetic pressure for trade reform provided by the USA, it is doubtful whether there would be much momentum behind trade reform and the Uruguay Round negotiations. Yet the USA is not a disinterested party. It has some clear and leading objectives, among them reduction of agricultural protection under the Common Agricultural Policy (CAP), and GATT-style coverage for trade in services and intellectual property rights. EC Europe is in principle committed to liberal trade, yet encompasses some strongly protectionist traditions and certainly does not wish to surrender too much protection for its agriculture. Its constituent member nations are often divided where trade policy issues are concerned, as the GATT negotiations demonstrate. Japan is anxious to preserve access for its manufacturing exports into rich country markets, while wishing at the same time to preserve its strong protection for its extremely uncompetitive agriculture, and also some of its own exotic (from a US perspective) political economic customs. The developing countries are uncertain of clear objectives for their group, yet certainly wish not to be neglected by more powerful parties, and with particular, and sometimes divergent, national interests, concerning, for example, fibre and food and manufacturing exports, and imports of services and intellectual property rights. Finally, the Cairns group promotes a reduction in agricultural protection.

If the EC seems different from other trade blocks, or from large nations with their trading arrangements with smaller partners, it is because it is a non-hegemonic union. It is not one large economy or country supplemented by smaller satellite economies. It is true that the strength of the West German economy stands out strongly against the background of some of its relatively weaker partners. Yet for the purpose of most decision making Germany is one of twelve EC member states, its influence magnified by population size and status more than directly by economic strength. No offence to Canada or Mexico is intended in stating that NAFTA is different in this respect. It is a USA plus neighbour economies block. However much diplomatic correctness may have preserved equal respect for all the NAFTA states in the negotiation of its internal rules, it remains the case that ease of access to the US market is what NAFTA is about, and that in the Uruguay Round negotiations it is the United States that represents NAFTA.

If the distinction between the non-hegemonic EC and hegemonic NAFTA is valid, it may be significant that where its exchange rate policy is concerned the EC found itself in effect adopting the opposite model. The European Monetary System (EMS) was not strictly asymmetric by design, but the relative strength of the Deutschemark, which far exceeded the relative strength even of the German economy, had the effect that one European country became the effective regulator of monetary policy for most of the other member states. Although German monetary policy performed that function, it was not formally required to do so. The implications and consequences of this inconsistency in block architecture will be further examined in Chapter 7.

Where blocks exist in any form, they will have to negotiate as blocks in the GATT reform process. Yet it would be a mistake to suppose that it is blocks that have generated the need for reform. GATT reform is needed because of persistent tendencies towards protectionism in the world economy.[4] If trade block formation is a leading cause of protectionism, then trade block formation is a serious problem. If trade block formation is less prevalent than may appear, the problem of the growth of protectionism still has to be addressed.

If the growth of protectionism and a tendency towards the formation of trade blocks are not the same thing, and they are not always closely associated, it is not a simple mistake to pair them, as is often done, in discussions of current problems of the world trading system. They are indeed leading issues, and there are some causal relations between the two cases.

On the one hand, protection may tend to promote blocks, because countries denied the benefits of general free trade may seek to gain at least the partial benefits of block membership. Less obvious is a causal connection between block formation and an increase in aggregate protection by the whole block, although such a connection is frequently asserted. From the theoretical point of view, the main reason blocks may be expected to be more protectionist is that their larger size implies that for them the level of optimum tariffs will be higher.[5] An equivalent way of putting the same point is to say that a group of countries forming a block coordinate their optimal tariff setting better because the external diseconomies caused when one country imports to the terms of trade of other countries are internalised.

It is difficult to discuss behaviour patterns of trade blocks as an empirical question. However many trade blocks there may be in the world, there are certainly very few. Hence generalisation based on empirical observation may be perilous. The external trade policy of the EC, for instance, which is protectionist in practice, and not only on account of the Common Agricultural Policy, may be the result of particular European circumstances rather than of a general tendency for trade blocks to behave in that way.

With few examples to examine it is not easy to be sure. If the empirical answer is obscure, the answer from theory, as will be seen below, is also ambiguous. While there is no inherent reason that a trade block has to be protectionist, whether it will be protectionist or not in fact is likely to depend on the objectives that the block chooses to pursue, and on the internal political and administrative forces that decide what those will be. Those latter factors are complex, as the EC again illustrates. It is not the case that the treaties forming European Community law and their amendments are protectionist as such, although their inward-looking orientation might give that impression. The way customs union and external tariff adjustment was implemented when the Community was formed was somewhat protectionist in effect (see Chapter 3 below). More importantly, by handing over the management of commercial policy to the EC Commission, the treaties laid the basis for protectionism to flourish in suitable circumstances. The subsequent administration of anti-dumping directives by the Commission has shown that this is not merely a theoretical problem. Apologists for the EC Commission will argue that, as an anti-dumping directive can always be vetoed in the Council of Ministers, that is where any blame should be laid. Proposed directives have been blocked in the Council but to rely on that mechanism is to ignore the whole thrust of the political economy of protection theory, which says that concentrated lobbying carries more political weight than do diffuse unorganised interests. The USA too makes wide use of anti-dumping tariffs.[6]

Notes

1 The relevant articles of the treaty are 123-127. See Rudden and Wyatt (1993), pp. 97-100 and 130.

2 For detailed information on the economics of the EC, see El-Agraa (1990).
3 See Frankel (1991).
4 See Bhagwati (1991, 1992), and Bhagwati and Patrick (1990).
5 See Johnson (1965), Krugman (1991a). See also Lawrence (1991).
6 On EC practices, see Hindley in Minford (1992).

CHAPTER 2

Protectionism, rules for trade and reform

2.1 The future of world trade

Central to the argument about trade blocks and their importance is the question of general world trading arrangements and their future. An alarmist view says that the world is breaking up into trade blocks, partly attributes block formation to the erosion of liberal trade, and holds that the erosion of liberal trade will itself be accelerated by block formation. A fortress Western Europe will confront an isolationist USA, with its satellite trading partners, and both will fight off Japanese attempts to sell them cheap manufactures, some of these assembled in Japanese-owned offshore factories.

Naturally this over-dramatic account of current developments is a parody. So far, despite many problems and worrying trends, world trade remains liberal in comparison with most past periods. There was never a time when everything was perfect, and the GATT, to tell the truth, has always been a decidedly imperfect set of arrangements. What has happened is that the relative importance of an unchanging list of GATT deficiencies has altered over time. These problems with the GATT include the following:[1]

- many developing countries were introduced to the GATT by ex-colonial sponsors, when, as the rules operated, they were subject to an unduly weak tariff discipline;
- the GATT is a rich countries' club, in the sense that most of its disputes are between the powerful industrial nations that dominate its operation;
- the exclusion of agriculture from the GATT, which was required to make ratification by the US Congress possible,[2] leaves one of the worst areas of trade restriction and resource misallocation untouched;

- the most favoured nation principle (MFN)[3] has been seriously eroded;
- the GATT focuses on tariffs, when quotas, voluntary export restraints and anti-dumping interventions (managed trade) are quantitatively more important interferences with the freedom of trade; and
- the GATT's coverage is too limited, excluding, for instance, trade in services, intellectual property rights, transnational investment, international cartels, competition policy and other features of modern economic life that importantly influence international exchange.

Roughly speaking, the items lower down the list have grown in importance over time relative to those higher up the list. Specifically, protectionism by less developed countries (LDCs) as a problem has greatly reduced. Today, LDCs generally set an example to an industrialised world that has grown more protectionist in practice. The fact that the GATT was dominated by rich countries mattered less while those countries inclined towards liberal trade and while they respected the MFN principle. Equally, when rich countries moved away from free trade practice, as they did with the GATT-illegal multi-fibre agreement, their lack of effective accountability became a serious problem.

Agricultural trade, while declining as a share of world trade, has grown in political importance, owing to growing conflict on this issue between the EC, the USA and other traders. A leading cause of the erosion of the MFN principle has been the conduct of its commercial policy by the EC, which now trades on an MFN basis with only a few countries, although these are large and include the USA and Japan. More generally, the proliferation of quotas and voluntary export restraints (VERs) by all major trading nations undermines the MFN principle and is probably illegal according to the GATT treaty – Article XI demands the general elimination of quantitative restrictions; Article XIII requires quantitative restrictions to be non-discriminatory (between nations); and, while Article XXIV admits various exceptions, they could not be interpreted to allow long-term quota restrictions against specific nations mainly on the ground that their competitiveness has become embarrassing. Finally, trade in services and other areas not well covered by the GATT has grown as a proportion of world trade.

To understand these trends it is important to bear in mind what the GATT was designed to do and what it never covered. The GATT agreement was never a complete free trade agreement. It accepted that the pressures on some governments to interfere with perfectly free trade would be irresistible and sought to regulate the conduct of such interference.[4] First, protection is required to be non-capricious. Increased protection is permitted only in response to serious adjustment problems for domestic producers, which seems to imply that it should be temporary. Secondly, and more importantly, there was the fundamental principle that protection should respect the MFN requirement, which required that protection should be non-discriminatory between different outside nations.

The treaty was nearly still-born, slipped into effect by executive device when the US Congress proved unwilling to ratify the treaty. As a consequence, the GATT system was never provided with an appropriate administrative apparatus. Thus the legal foundations of the GATT are shaky enough to keep international lawyers disputing forever. When account is taken of all these facts, that it worked as well as it did is impressive. Consider that the legal form of the GATT is summarized by a useful term of the art, 'functioning of the GATT system', and that this abbreviates itself with singular appropriateness to FOGS. Like democracy, the GATT has little to recommend it, except that every alternative is much worse.[5]

Cynics will say that the GATT system worked because the post-war world was booming and trade flourished in a way that did good for all the major trading nations. Then they were willing to cut tariffs in coordinated fashion as in the Kennedy and Tokyo rounds. On a pessimistic view, it can be argued that the trade climate has been steadily turning colder, that the resulting political economic stresses have already severely damaged the system and that worse is to come. Now that GATT reform is badly needed, this view would maintain, it will be nearly impossible to achieve. And those villainous trade blocks will play a leading role in worsening the situation and in blocking the achievement of the required reform.

This negative view begs the question about the role that will be played by trade blocks by assuming that trade blocks will wish to interfere with the freedom of inter-block trade as far as regulations permit. That is far from obvious. Inter-block trade accounts for about half of world trade, so it is very important. Moreover, inter-block trade is probably more important than its simple weight in total trade would indicate, because trade that moves long distances will often confer particularly large gains resulting from differences in comparative advantage. It is plausible, as an instance of this view, that Britain gains more from the import of bananas than it gains from importing French apples, and that could be true even if the values of the two import bills were to be the same.

2.2 Trade negotiation

There is always a balance of forces between the pressures for protection, on the one side, and the benefits of trade as perceived by governments, or other advocates, on the other side. That principle applies as well to inter-block trade as it does where more local exchange is concerned. This assumes that non-conflicting tariffs (optimal tariffs) have already been established.[6] From a theoretical point of view, as will be seen below, it is not obvious that gains from local exchange strictly need to conflict with the benefits of trade between blocks, although the problems of administrating the ideal outcome are admittedly complex.

It would be wrong to suppose that the case for taking advantage of the gains from inter-block trade will make itself felt independently of the institutions that govern the conduct of international trade. Perhaps the easiest way of explaining the point is to note that the establishment of rules can be the mechanism for sustaining cooperation in the type of situation in which the non-cooperative outcome would involve excessive protection, rational from the point of view of the individual country acting alone, but destructive of the national interests of all. Modelled as a game, in the sense of game theory,[7] liberal trade can resemble the regulation of motor vehicle parking. It is no proof that parking rules are not to the general benefit that they may be a source of profound irritation to the individual motorist looking for somewhere to leave a car. Indeed, even that particular motorist may be a beneficiary generally from rules that restrict and irritate on a particular occasion.

Why negotiate rules rather than negotiating each trade and exchange on its own terms? The answer that a once-for-all negotiation of rules will save negotiation costs and uncertainties of the outcome may well suffice in itself. Another angle would see rules as the implementation of the cooperative solution to a game. To explain the character of this game is to throw great light on the way in which gains from trade and the convenience of protection interact and oppose each other. In many simple models to be found in international economics textbooks, zero protection is the best policy for each country even if other countries protect. Models of that type can throw no light on the design and function of rules to enforce liberal trade. There is no need for rules in those models because free trade would be self-enforcing.[8]

Even if one concedes free trade to be the best thing for all countries in the long run, and with suitable systems of compensation applied, it may be that the short-run political–economic interest of each country is to cheat by imposing some protection. Then a game similar to the prisoners' dilemma arises.[9] Both (or all) countries cheating makes both (or all) worse off than with no protection

The conclusions that may be drawn from the initial consideration of the state of GATT and of the implications of block formation are that GATT may need updating in a way that takes into account blocks and their effects, but that neither blocks as such, nor inevitable protectionist pressures, imply that this could not in principle be done to the great benefit of all the parties involved. To say that it could be done in principle is not to say that it will be done. To understand the barriers to rational international trade reform, the argument has to appreciate the sources and causes of political pressures in favour of protection, because these can be very powerful.

Not all the pressures are of one kind. Sometimes the motive force behind the pressure originates in the government or administration itself. One case has been called the non-economic objective. The idea is that the administration makes use of protection to steer the allocation of resources towards a direction determined, not by a wish to improve on the allocation of resources as such, but rather by some other aim. This is most imprecise and it is doubtful if it can be made precise. The difficulty is of distinguishing the non-economic aim clearly from the general aim of improving the operation of the market system.[10] Examples illustrate the issues well. Take the wish to preserve farming as a way of life in industrial countries, which is frequently invoked in the justification of agricultural protection. If this is a non-economic objective, it is because farming as a way of life is a non-market good, even if we concede that it is a good. And that does not seem adequate because several economic goods, such as freedom from acid rain, are of their nature also non-market goods.

Obviously only governments can initiate and sustain protection, just as only governments can remove or reduce it. We should take protection to include not just the exclusion of imports, but also the promotion of exports, as similar principles apply in the two cases. The extensive literature on the political economy of protection[11] mainly sees governments as reactive to political pressures from affected interest groups, and there is much sense in that view. Even when governments assert that they are themselves the author of a scheme inspired by high and abstract considerations, this may be questioned. It is significant in this connection that no government works to promote farming as a way of life that is not, as it happens, the target of powerful interest pressures from existing farmers. It would seem easy to dismiss governments' own aims as icing on a simple economic interest cake.

The issues are not very different where export promotion is at issue. Again, governments that appear to be active, to be pursuing grand designs above the heads of voters, may be seen on closer consideration to be protecting the same sort of interests – the interests of factors, especially specific factors, and the interests of rent seekers – the same type of interest as is defended by import exclusion policies. Where economies of scale are important, however, the simple distinction between import-excluding policies and export promotion may break down.

Take the European Airbus project as an example. Surely this is a case of export promotion actively pursued by the agents of the governments that have supplied funding for the scheme. True, the salesman closing a deal in the USA looks like an ordinary commercial sales agent. Yet as the budget constraint for the scheme is quite soft, and governments are picking up the bill, the salesman should be seen as an indirect agent of governments. The reason for the export-promoting activity in this case is not that the governments concerned place a value on exporting aircraft as such. Rather the industry can succeed, and hence associated specific factors and rent-seeking interests can be protected, and a government objective of having an aircraft industry succeed, only if the industry is enabled to operate on a sufficiently large scale, and that can only happen if there is a large volume of exports.

2.3 Gainful trade that hurts

Economists typically assert that most interferences with free trade are inefficient in the sense that the benefits that they confer on specific parties could be more cheaply realised by alternative policy devices. The idea is good but there are problems with applying it and these go some way towards explaining why its impact on policy makers has been limited.

Gainful trade can hurt some parties. The best-known instance of this is the Stolper–Samuelson effect.[12] Allowing in an import lowers the demand for factors of production used intensively in its manufacture and releases them for the production of higher-value products. There is a clear national gain, in this example at least. For the gain to be realised through a market system, however, prices have to adjust, including factor prices.

The Stolper–Samuelson argument says that these factor price changes are large compared with the output price changes and that one factor at least must lose regardless of its consumption pattern. The argument was used to explain why labour tended to lobby for the protection of labour-intensive activities. The model is not quite accurate in its predictions. The prediction that factors, say labour and capital, will tend to lobby on different sides of the argument for and against protection is not in accord with the facts. The evidence shows that the different factors tend to line up together in favour of protection when there is lobbying in that direction.[13]

The main explanation for this last observation is that factors are much less mobile than the Stolper–Samuelson model posits. Capital in particular is specific to the sectors to which it has been allocated, in the short run at least. In any case, adjustment poses costs on some or all factors. The efficiency of free trade argument says that the losers could be compensated by the gainers. But, to follow up this advice, governments would have to allocate scarce tax revenue to the payment of compensation, for the non-distortionary lump-sum taxes of the textbook are never available, and the special gain-creaming taxes that would be needed to divert the monetary benefits to the gainers are also well outside the realm of possibility. Much protection is a budgetarily inexpensive way of avoiding harm to entrenched interests. That still greater harm to others results may not be reflected in offsetting political pressure if the losers are many and dispersed. An obvious instance of this case would be the protection afforded to fibre and garment producers in industrial countries. The gains are concentrated among a limited number of factory owners and some workers, while the costs are widely dispersed and hard for those suffering them to quantify.

Competitive strategic planning of international trade is illustrated by the European Commission's ill-starred scheme for promoting a European standard for high definition television (HDTV), which was openly designed to make the European market less accessible for Japanese manufacturers. The scheme has now collapsed. Even had it persisted, it is doubtful whether it would have protected the European market, leave alone placing European industry in a better position to compete with Japanese manufacturers in third country markets. The formal economic modelling of this type of case has usually emphasised the shifting of profits to the country or block that provides an environment in which a large high-return-to-scale manufacturing activity flourishes.

Yet that is only part of an argument, not always well developed, that can be distilled from the statements of politicians and administrators. In short, this says that opportunities for manufacturing employment are an important national value in their own right. The idea seems to be that high-tech manufacturing will be a dynamic sector from which important future rents will flow. Notice that a reference to rents takes the argument to wider ground than is covered by profit shifting alone. Imagine, for instance, that well-paying jobs will be provided by the industry.

For a small industry one might say that a high wage is only the opportunity cost of a type of labour that would otherwise earn a similar wage elsewhere. Indeed the higher the wage the higher the opportunity cost. For huge projects claiming to affect the whole character of the national economy, however, wage rates and employment opportunities are determined in part by the grand strategy, and to understand the thinking behind this type of programme, which is often modelled on a stylised account of Japanese post-war success, one has to appreciate that point.

This is not necessarily to concede that Japanese success is to be attributed to far-sighted strategic protection and export promotion, or to allow, even if that is the case, that this particular organisational and administrative technology will travel well. In examining the pressures towards protection we need to understand the lines along which influential people are thinking and to see that ideas that may have little value in practice are not necessarily simple fallacies. The HDTV example also illustrates how the instruments favoured for protection and export promotion reflect a view of the nature of the trade problem. If governments have grown increasingly less willing to legislate a simple environment for international exchange, relying mainly on relatively simple and stable tariff schedules, it is because they view trade more and more as amenable to a more reactive, strategic and detailed management.

2.4 Managed trade

The GATT is in disarray, no question. While industrial countries have tariff levels as modest as has been seen since the First World War, tariff rates as such have become increasingly irrelevant. Today trade is regulated by quotas, anti-dumping directives, minimum price restrictions on imports, the Multi-Fibre Agreement, voluntary export restraints, foreign content restrictions, safety and standards regulations; and, watch this space, whatever politicians and legislators will dream up next. The tariff seems almost charmingly unsophisticated in comparison with that armory: like a bow and arrow set beside a modern automatic weapon. In fact there is nothing charming about tariffs, which can have devastating effects on trade and welfare. There are, however, reasons why the nature of trade restriction has tended to change over time. Some have to do with the operation of the GATT itself, others are associated with precisely the kinds of cases and institutions that the new trade theory is designed to cover.

It would not be accurate to say that non-tariff restrictions have proved popular because the GATT prohibits tariffs but permits other kinds of trade restriction. The GATT does not prohibit tariffs – it regulates their application.[14] However, central to that regulation is the famous most favoured nation principle, and the MFN rule may partly explain why other kinds of restriction have been preferred to tariffs. Trade restrictions are very often responses to crises: domestic producers are being hurt by imports and they are screaming. What are you going to do about it, Minister? More and more these crises arise because the exports of one or a small group of nations are penetrating the domestic market and the authorities want a policy that will target those exports directly. Not only does a general tariff have that effect indirectly, it might even be counter-productive. A general tariff raises the domestic price level for the good more than does a nation-specific tariff, and that could provide an incentive to the more competitive exporters to get round the tariff, for instance by cutting their prices.

By cutting their prices. That simple phrase conveys an important assumption. Small competitive producers cannot deliberately alter their prices to offset the effects of a tariff, although notice that a competitive equilibrium can produce the same effect on the foreign price. When foreign producers are moved down their supply curves, a lower foreign price results. In the competitive case, however, the response of the foreign price must be associated with a fall in the quantity exported. When foreign firms are large and behave strategically, they may decide to hold on to their market share by cutting the price at which they export to the home market to offset the effect of the tariff on the domestic price.

Where it is an exchange rate change that is offset by exporters' pricing policy, the term usually employed is exchange rate pass-through.[15] However, the same considerations that could lead imperfectly competitive foreign producers not to pass through an exchange rate appreciation in their country's currency (relative to the currency of the foreign market) fully into foreign prices apply equally to tariff changes. Where a country is embarrassed by cheap imports, say of Japanese motor vehicles, the most favoured nation principle may be viewed as quite irrelevant to its concerns, and a general tariff may seem to miss the relevant target. Worse, a general tariff may make matters more difficult if political pressures are reacting to imports from a particular country. For the tariff will raise the domestic price of the good, offsetting some of the import discouragement caused by the tariff itself. Should the supply of the producer who was causing discontent be relatively price inelastic, that producer will take an increased share of the import market, which may not make everyone happy.

2.5 Customs unions and the GATT

Originally the MFN principle was not designed with the kind of intervention that I have been discussing explicitly in mind. The immediate post-war world was still a colonial, or recently colonial, world, and one of the considerations that influenced the GATT architects was the wish to legislate against the world arranging itself into restrictive trading blocks built around colonial countries and their ex-colonies, particularly, and around regions as well.

Yet the GATT made an important exception for customs unions, although these involve trade discrimination. Essentially the authors of the GATT took the view that a customs union is a super-nation for the purpose of applying the MFN principle. Why did the GATT allow customs unions? In this connection it is worth quoting from Article XXIV of the treaty:

> The contracting parties recognize the desirability of increasing freedom of trade by the development, through voluntary agreements, of closer integration between the economies of the countries party to such agreements. They also recognize that the purpose of a customs union or of a free trade area should be to facilitate trade between the constituent territories and not to raise barriers to the trade of other contracting parties with such territories.

and later:

> duties and other regulations [of the customs union] shall not on the whole be higher or more restrictive than the general incidence

of the duties and regulations of commerce [previously] applicable.[16]

In this context it is illuminating to notice that customs unions and free trade areas have proved to be popular. While protectionism is undoubtedly popular also, trade isolationism is not, and all countries have been keen either to join trading blocks, or at least not to be excluded from them. This tendency to block formation must spend its force well short of the whole world, or we would witness a movement towards a world-wide trading block, which would be world free trade, which we do not.

There is an increasing returns to scale aspect to this, with the importance of participating in a large market carrying great weight, because it gives home producers the benefit of scale as exporters, and because it gives home purchasers of imports benefits of low costs from its suppliers. The standard neoclassical points, however, explain much of what has to be explained. Trade is gainful on account of differences in comparative advantage. To have it diminished, as will happen if a country finds itself on the wrong side of trade diversion, is an unpleasant outcome that any rational country takes care to avoid.

What a trading block provides is the same as the original GATT provided – reciprocity. Although theoretical models may show unilateral free trade to be beneficial, most countries would mostly like the benefits of free trade access to other markets while reserving for themselves the right to protect their own markets selectively against imports. In other words, they would like to free-ride on free trade arrangements. When tariffs were the most important protectionist instrument, the GATT effectively prohibited the grossest free-riding at least. As protectionist devices have become different and more sophisticated, however, GATT rules have become less efficient as anti-free-riding devices. One attraction of the trading block is that it promises the possibility of establishing and policing free trade, on a local basis at least, with effective reciprocity. It is tempting precisely to reverse the conventional wisdom that says that the GATT is breaking down mainly or partly because of the growth of trading blocks, and say, rather, that a major impetus behind the growth of trading blocks has been the weakening of the GATT as an effective system for regulating international trade. Trading blocks are GATT substitutes to some extent. Of course, in answering a slogan one should not descend to the level of sloganising. The sources of trading block growth are several and complex, and certainly include political objectives, as well as political and social concords.

This is obvious in the case of the EC, where the original motivations were powerfully political and internationally strategic. Even so, granted the point, the Communities were economic agreements governing economic arrangements. If the true overwhelming objective of European unity was the avoidance of a future European war, then it is interesting that the war-blocking method selected (or at least the part of the plan that it proved easiest to put into effect) was predominantly closer economic union.

Another point is that 'do-it-yourself' free trade arrangements may require political and cultural concord. Otherwise we arrive at the counter-intuitive conclusion that where the GATT fails the whole world can set in place better Pareto-improving arrangements. It would be rather similar to the simple proof that says that an allocation in the core of a game has to be Pareto efficient. Proof: a core allocation cannot be blocked (improved on for all) by any coalition of players relying on their own resources. A coalition of all the players can block a Pareto-inefficient allocation. QED[17]

The argument needs to be developed to avoid such simplistic conclusions. Broadly there are two types of trading blocks, the hegemonic type and the symmetrical type, though these are stylised extremes. The hegemonic block could be illustrated by the NAFTA. It is centred on one overarching large nation of massive power, the USA in this case, and it will look chiefly to that nation for the regulation of internal trade at least. The symmetrical type is illustrated by the EC. There is no single dominant power and rules for internal trade have to be arrived at by a consensual/political process. Although the second type sounds, and is, more complicated to govern, neither is easy. Yet perhaps difficulties of administration lead to some benefits. The EC with its single market has established rules for trade that are tighter and more explicit than the GATT ever managed to establish.

The GATT has lost effectiveness and needs reform. Various proposals as to how this should be done have been canvassed. The USA is the leading maker of ideas and the driving force behind the Uruguay Round negotiations. Important contributions to the debate are made by the GATT organisation itself, by leading trading nations such as Japan, by the EC Commission and the Cairns group, as well as by individual countries, particularly on issues that they identify as of particular importance for their own trading interests. There is a huge diversity of philosophy and of interest. The complexity of modern techniques of trade management, and deficiencies in the original treaty, make it seem doubtful how far a new treaty could effectively police trade on a world-wide basis.

As the reform of the GATT concerns this volume only in so far as the trade block as such makes a difference, it is appropriate to keep the argument brief. For books have been written, and more will be, on GATT reform.[18] The following objectives should define a minimal agenda for the reform of the law of international trade. That some items are included in the list that have not been proposed for the Uruguay Round discussions is a measure both of the difficulties that the whole exercise must face, and also of the fact that the commitment of leading negotiators to true free trade, however enthusiastic it may be in general, remains qualified in important particulars.

1. coverage of agriculture, trade in services and intellectual property rights;
2. regulation of quotas, anti-dumping and VERs;
3. regulation of export promotion by subsidy and weak competition control;
4. a globalisation of anti-dumping measures, with an effective appeals mechanism, and the prohibition of the most outlandish dumping, including EC foodstuffs dumping;
5. regulation of protection under the cover of product specification, safety and health regulation, or environmental objectives.

Calling this list minimal is intended to be provocative, for it will surely appear as absurdly over-ambitious from the point of view of political feasibility. What the list shows is what would have to be done to bring the GATT up to date and to repair major deficiencies that experience of the original treaty in operation has exposed. One lesson of the last type is surely that a trade treaty needs to empower some body to administer its rules, because reliance on individual governments to invoke treaty obligations from others will not suffice by itself. For one thing, it will always leave small and weak countries, such as Hong Kong, helpless against the threat of having their trade mugged by more powerful countries screaming ‘anti-dumping’. Similarly, if environmental or similar restrictions on trade are to be admitted, there needs to be some kind of court with the power to declare some of these interventions illegal; otherwise, in practice, it will be possible to bar almost any import.

Should a small country consider taking legal action against a large trading nation, or the EC, through the GATT process for wrongly excluding its imports, as has occasionally happened, it is not only up against the huge resources for defending such actions commanded by a rich party. It is also disabled by wording of Article VI,[19] the vagueness of which almost seems to invite abuse. Dumping is defined as: 'introducing products into the commerce of another country at *less than the normal value of the products*' (italics added).[20]

If the list of requirements laid out above seems absurdly long and ambitious, its purpose is partly mischievous. By indicating how difficult it would be to establish liberal world trade on a legislative/treaty basis, it prepares the ground for a radically different approach to be given serious consideration. Despite the massive and evident problems for international trade in the modern world, trading blocks have come into being and are being developed and extended. The lesson may be that the entire world is too large an area on which to establish the most free trade that is possible. To put it another way, the simple idea that customs unions or free trade areas are a first step in the right direction may not be exactly right as economic theory, for it depends upon union design, as will be seen below, but could yet be entirely correct as a description of political administrative feasibility.

If the trading block works as an institution with good generation and survival performance, it might plausibly be made the basis for the design of the world trading system. One might even wish to promote the organisation of countries not at present included in a trading block, especially numerous developing countries, either into new, probably regional, trading blocks in their own right, or into satellite relationships with the existing major trading blocks.

That will not dispose of the world trade problem because trade between blocks is very important. For the outside world to be denied the benefits of Japanese design and production skills, or to lose the advantages of US climatic endowment, land abundance and agro-technique, where food is concerned, and so on, would be heavy costs. Once, however, the trading block is accepted, not as a sinister development that we would really like to stamp on, but as part of the right answer, we can then turn our attention to rules for inter-block trade.

The objectives of the last rules would need to be less ambitious than would be appropriate for rules designed to regulate the whole of world trade. Locally, within blocks, self-policing would regulate trade, and we would be looking only for rules to encourage inter-block trade and to prohibit policies excessively harmful to those outside the block. These are general ideas. In order to see how far they might take us, we first need to develop more theory about how a customs union or a trade block functions, and that is the subject of the next two chapters.

Notes

1 On problems in the GATT and for the Uruguay Round negotiations, see Baldwin and Richardson (1988, 1991); Curzon-Price (1992) and Winters (1990).
2 In fact the US Congress never ratified the treaty; see below.
3 Articles I and II of the treaty refer. See GATT (1986).
4 On the trade philosophy implicit in the GATT, see Krugman (1992).
5 On the GATT and its development, see Jackson (1990).
6 See Johnson (1965) and Corden (1974), Ch. 7.
7 For a short review of game theory ideas, see Ch. 11 of Tirole (1988).
8 Negotiation typically reflects the view that countries like exports and dislike imports unless balanced by exports. Krugman (1992) calls this 'GATT-think'. See also Cooper and Massell (1965).
9 See Tirole (1988), p. 426.
10 On non-economic objectives and trade, see Corden (1974), Ch. 2.
11 See Corden (1984), p. 10 and Magee, Brock and Young (1989).
12 See Stolper and Samuelson (1941).
13 Stephen Magee (1978) attempts a theoretical explanation of the fact that factors tend to lobby in unison.
14 See Robertson (1992).
15 See Dixit (1989) and Froot and Klemperer (1988).
16 GATT (1986), pp. 412.
17 See Varian (1984), pp. 235-9.
18 See Bhagwati (1991) and Jackson (1990).
19 See Gatt (1986), p. 10.
20 On the issue of dumping, see Yarrow (1987).

CHAPTER 3

Customs union theory

3.1 Basic concepts and tariff averaging

The GATT is indulgent with regard to customs union formation, provided that external protection is not increased. This philosophy of customs union formation was partly based on a belief that it would be a step on the road towards global free trade. Also, by not legislating what would be required to hold the extent of protection for the aggregate of customs union members constant, the authors of the GATT implicitly took the view that not increasing the extent of external protection is easy and simple to determine. When the original EC was formed it adopted arithmetic tariff averaging, which meant that the common external tariff for each product was set at the unweighted arithmetic average of the pre-union tariff rates charged by the individual countries for that product. For a specific product some member countries raised their tariff rates, others lowered them; but on balance it seemed to average out to an unchanged degree of protection.[1] Later-joining countries adopted the existing common external tariffs of the union. The reason for the EC adopting tariff averaging was perhaps to solve an awkward problem simply and directly, and to make the new EC less provocative in terms of GATT legality and trade offence to other nations, especially the USA.

The idea that a customs union is necessarily a step on the road to free trade, and the notion that any simple formula can ensure a constant degree of external protection, are far too simple, as will be shown below. Yet each contains a kernel of truth. One of the tasks of this chapter will be to extract the conditions under which the benefits of increased trade between the members of a customs union can be captured without harm to outsiders, and the rates at which the common external tariffs have to set – 'averaged' – to achieve that end.

The idea that tariff averaging, defined as an arithmetic average of member nation tariff rates, corresponds in some sense to protection neutrality is simplistic. It is hard to think of a serious argument in favour of strict arithmetic averaging. Why should the tariffs of small nations carry an equal weight with the tariffs of large nations? Split any nation into two and its tariffs, whatever they may be, low or high, carry double weight. Arithmetic tariff averaging cannot make sense. Later in this chapter the emphasis is placed on a special case of a customs union not harming the outside world. This is the customs union that chooses its common external tariffs so that the aggregate of its members' trade with the outside world is the same as it was without the customs union. To discover which tariffs common to all member nations produce the same external trade as the various different national tariffs that the member nations charged before the union was formed is an algebraic exercise, which is solved in the appendix to this chapter. What emerges from that exercise is the conclusion that the formula for the single common tariff that has the same effect as a diversity of tariffs does not show that tariff to be an average of the previous tariffs, not even a weighted average. Yet certain features of a weighted average are replicated in the correct formula. For instance, the tariffs of large countries carry additional weight, as they do not do when a simple arithmetic formula is applied.

The extensive theoretical work on customs unions of Viner, Lipsey, Meade, Johnson, Scitovsky, Vanek and others[2] did not directly address the question of the choice of the common external tariffs for a customs union. This was not because these authors were unaware of the significance of that choice. Rather they were interested in investigating the results of simple tariff averaging, particularly for the special case of tariff averaging in which the countries that make up the customs union all start with the same tariffs and keep them for trade with the outside world. This was a natural orientation of their theorising given that they were responding to the formation of the early European Economic Community of six members, which precisely followed the rule of setting its common external tariff to the arithmetic average of member tariff rates.

The work of these theorists established an implicit criticism of tariff averaging by making it clear that a customs union may divert trade, which means re-routing it to inside the union, contrary to the requirements of world efficiency, as well as creating trade, which means realising the benefits of increased trade between its own members.[3] The literature on customs union theory is daunting. There are many models, many assumptions, many cases. Even so, a relatively small number of essential ideas capture the most important things that have to be understood.

In an early and essential contribution, Viner showed that a customs union could be trade diverting or trade creating, or either or both in any proportion. A very simple model illustrates the idea. The example that follows is of a type that is very well known. Despite the familiarity of the model, however, it is useful to lay out an example, particularly because for later reference attention needs to be drawn to the way in which income and income distribution are treated. Also, the numerous extensions and adaptations of this root model define the field of customs union theory.

3.2 The Viner model: An example

There are three countries, called Arcadia, Bella and Extra – denoted A, B and E, for short. In all three countries many small producers produce two goods, which are called Bread and Wine, from one factor, called Labour, under constant returns to scale. Obviously the particular names for goods and factors are employed to make the example colourful, and no significance attaches to them. Bread and wine are consumed in the same fixed proportions 1:1 in all countries. The labour requirements per unit of output for the countries, and their labour supplies, are given in the table.

Initially, both A and B have a 25% tariff on the import of wine. For A this is not large enough to defeat the comparative advantage of E in producing wine. The price of wine in terms of bread in A will be 1.25. Let the equilibrium consumptions of bread and wine in A be (x,x). This will cost $2.25x$ and will equal the amount available for expenditure, $100 + T = 100 + 25x$, where T is tariff revenue. Hence equilibrium will satisfy:

$$2.25x = 100 + 0.25x \tag{3.1}$$

which is satisfied by $x = 50$.

Table 3.1 Labour requirements and supplies in the Viner example

Bread	Wine	Labour	Countries
1	1.25	100	Arcadia
1	1.20	100	Bella
1	1.00	200	Extra

In B the price of domestically-produced wine will be 1.2. The 25% tariff is high enough to protect wine production in B. Imported wine from E would cost 1.25, whereas home-produced wine will cost 1.2 in terms of bread. With an income of 100 and no tariff revenue this buys a balanced consumption basket (45.46,45.46). In E, equilibrium consumption is (100,100). A produces only bread, B both bread and wine for its own consumption. E's consumption is (100,100). Hence E imports 50 units of bread from A and exports 50 units of wine to A. Because both A's and E's producers are numerous and competitive, the price at which trade of bread for wine takes place is determined by the relative price of the country that produces both goods and trades, Extra.

Now let Arcadia and Bella form a customs union. It looks like a good idea for wine consumers in A, as the bread price of wine will fall to 1.2. However, tariff revenue disappears and A's consumption falls to B's previous level (45.46,45.46). A loses; B is unaffected; as is E, whose cost conditions set world prices. This is pure trade diversion. Notice how the income effect, because of the loss of tariff revenue, plays an essential role in the welfare loss resulting from trade diversion. If we just look at prices in A, the customs union appears to be definitely gainful, for it cuts the cost of imported wine. That we always need to look at both the income effect and the price effect of a change in trade arrangements is a point that will be encountered more than once again.

The example is only that, an example, but one can see at once how to change it to get different results. It was assumed, for instance, that E's production cost for wine would set the world wine price, and it was because it did so that trade diversion caused by the customs union did no harm to E, the outside world. If the price of wine were to have been higher, then trade diversion would harm E and we would have perhaps a more typical case. The assumption that bread and wine are consumed in strictly fixed proportions rules out the important substitution effect. The customs union, as we have just seen, lowered the relative cost of wine in A, but this brought no benefit as the ability to substitute into wine consumption from bread consumption was absent. If we allow substitution, the customs union brings consumption benefits, which are a type of trade creation. More generally, change the numbers in the example, and trade creation predominates. That is about as far as simple two-good examples will take us.

To see the substitution effect operating, keep the numbers of the example but, instead of assuming consumption in fixed proportions, suppose that in each country a representative consumer has a utility function:

$$b^{0.444}.w^{0.556} \tag{3.2}$$

where b and w are respectively the quantities of bread and wine consumed. The particular values of the exponents of b and w are chosen so that the two goods will be consumed in the proportions 1:1 prior to the formation of the customs union. This allows direct comparison with the original model in which the two goods are always consumed in the proportion 1:1, regardless of relative prices. With the consumer's income in terms of bread equal to I, and p the price of wine in terms of bread, the indirect utility function is:

$$(0.444I)^{0.444}\left(0.556\frac{I}{p}\right)^{0.556}; \tag{3.3}$$

and, when the price of wine is 1.25, demands for bread and wine satisfy:

$$\begin{aligned} b &= 0.444I \\ w &= 0.556\frac{I}{1.25} \end{aligned} \tag{3.4}$$

As income is the sum of bread produced plus tariff revenue, we have:

$$I = 100 + 0.25(0.556)\frac{I}{1.25} \tag{3.5}$$

and the equations are satisfied by $I = 112.5$, $b = 50$ and $w = 50$.

Thus, by construction, the consumer demands in Arcadia, prior to the formation of the customs union, are (50,50), as in the original fixed-proportions consumption model. The utility level is calculated by substituting the values just obtained into the indirect utility function to obtain $U = 50$, as would be expected because U is 50 to the power 0.444 times 50 to the power 0.556. With the customs union the price of wine falls to 1.2, as before. Now:

$$I = 100 + 0.2(0.556)\frac{I}{1.2};$$

which gives $I = 110.2$. Demands for bread and wine are respectively 48.93 and 51.06. Utility is 50.1, just a shade more than without the customs union. The trade diversion of wine production into high-cost Bella is just more than offset by the advantage that the consumers of Arcadia obtain by substituting in their consumption in favour of cheaper wine. Hence the idea that the customs union could benefit wine consumers by giving them cheaper wine was not nonsense. Of course the example is only an example. When production inefficiencies, caused by trade diversion, and consumer substitution benefits pull against each other, the net outcome can go either way.

Another extension of and qualification to Viner's original argument was provided by Meade, who pointed out that trade diversion does not have to take the form of the diversion of the export of a specific good from one country to another. Suppose that our three countries produce three goods: bread, beer and wine, with comparative advantage lying respectively with A, B and E; so much so that B cannot produce wine and E cannot produce beer. Then a customs union formed by the integration of A and B will encourage beer consumption in A and lower demand for wine. It is just like trade diversion but no particular trade is diverted.

This brief sketch of received customs union theory only hints at the richness of the taxonomy that can be developed. Some of the complexities spring from the fact that the theory typically addresses a model in which:

- the membership of the union is arbitrary (politically determined);
- the union is not required to be optimal, from the economic point of view, for all or any of its members;
- the initial external tariffs of the union members are also arbitrary, and are adjusted, if at all, only in some simple way (e.g. tariff averaging).

Much of this is realistic, say for the original European union, the motivation for much of the early work. The European Common Market in its original form did keep its existing external tariffs, applying tariff averaging. Later, as the EC enlarged by adding further members, the joining members were required to adopt the common external tariff of the existing Community members. As for the most part later-joining members had higher external tariffs than the common external tariff at the time, a mild liberalisation of trade was implied at that stage, at least for manufactured goods.

3.3 The tariff-compensating customs union

The customs union that benefits its members by virtue of its trade creation and does not harm the rest of the world is the ideal of traditional customs union theory, which shows that, for the case of

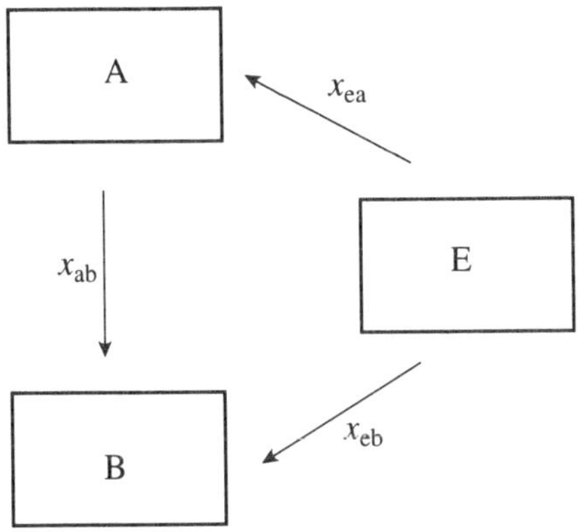

Figure 3.1

given external tariffs, the ideal will be achieved or not according to the particular patterns of comparative advantage, substitutability, and so on. Why not design a customs union to make it ideal? It took trade theorists a long time to examine this idea in detail. Ohyama (1972) introduced the concept of a tariff-compensating customs union, a union that would set 'its common external tariffs so as to preserve the same volume and composition of net trade with the rest of the world as occurred before it was formed'. The elementary proposition of Kemp and Wan (1976) embodies the same idea. Although it emerged from the press later, the Kemp–Wan argument is so elegant that it is followed closely here. The original is highly recommended, embodying as it does most features of the ideal economics paper: about two pages long; no explicit mathematics; yet a beautiful precise argument.

Figure 3.1 shows trade flows in a three-country world prior to the formation of a customs union involving A and B. Trade flows are shown as net flow vectors, which is why only three are involved. Thus x_{ab} is an unsigned vector of exports from A to B. If B exports net to A, then x_{ab} has a negative value for the corresponding component. The idea of the Kemp–Wan theorem is that A and B will adjust their economies and the trade x_{ab} between themselves as desired, while holding constant the sum of their trades with E; that is: $x_{ea} + x_{eb}$.

The proof of the Kemp–Wan theorem appeals to a known result in general equilibrium theory, the so-called Fundamental Theorem of Welfare Economics (FTWE).[4] For that reason the paper's extreme brevity perhaps suggests a simpler argument than is in fact involved. By

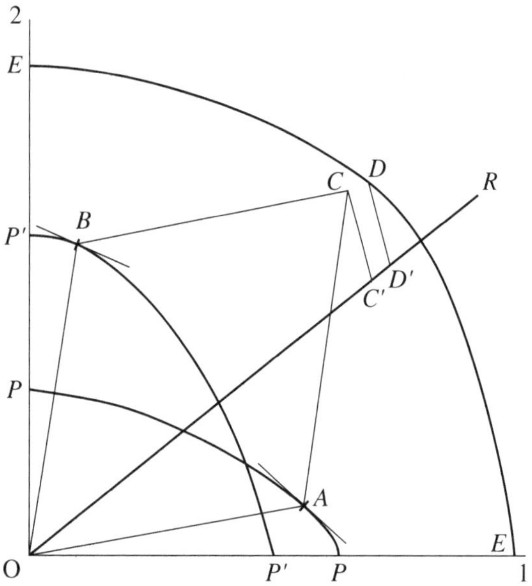

Figure 3.2

invoking the powerful FTWE, with the proof of which readers are assumed to be familiar, or for which they must look elsewhere, the argument cuts the demonstration of the result down to a short and decisive verbal argument. As the mathematical proof of the FTWE uses a separating hyperplane theorem, the entire argument, were it laid out fully, would not be mathematically trivial. Even so, it remains quite intuitive. The result is first demonstrated by means of a diagram, for a very simple case. Then the intuition of a more general case is explained. Finally, the general mathematical proof, which invokes the FTWE, will be explained, as in the original Kemp–Wan paper.

A diagrammatic depiction of the result is shown in Figure 3.2. There are only two goods in the economy and production possibility frontiers for Arcadia and Bella are shown as *PP* and *P'P'* respectively. To keep the specification of equilibrium simple, consumers of Arcadia and Bella all consume Goods 1 and 2 in the same fixed proportions shown by the slope of the ray O*R*. Initially Arcadia and Bella are separate and charge tariffs and at different rates. Hence their initial producer prices are different, as is shown on the figure by the fact that the slopes of the tangents to the production possibility curves at *A* and *B* are different.

The production of the two countries together is given by completing the parallelogram to arrive at *C*. *C* is inside the frontier *EE* (*E* standing for efficiency, not for Extra). This is because *EE* is the production possibility frontier of Arcadia and Bella taken together, which is the outer limit of all parallelograms formed from two points on respectively the frontiers *PP* and *P'P'*. *EE* is reached only when the slopes of the two frontiers are equal. When production is at *C*, consumers consume at *C'* on the ray O*R*, and this involves trade with Extra from *C* to *C'*, with terms of trade given by that slope. This is assumed possible, for the figure depicts an equilibrium.

Now Arcadia and Bella form a customs union and move to common producer prices and efficient production. The point *D* on the frontier *EE* satisfies two properties: it is efficient; and the line from *D* to the ray O*R* at *D'* is the same in slope and length as the line *CC'*. Hence consumers in Arcadia and Bella consume at *D'*, a welfare improvement, while trade with Extra is unaffected.

To support the diagrammatic demonstration of the Kemp–Wan result, we may tell the story in informal terms. Rather than calculating the non-trade-affecting common external tariff, imagine that foreign trade is all handled by a public organisation – call it the foreign trade ministry. Let this be true both for Arcadia and for Bella, each of which will have its own independent foreign trade ministry. Initially these ministries import less from the outside world than would be the case with free trade. They auction these quantities on the domestic market and the prices that they fetch define implicit tariffs. The foreign trade ministries do not trade with each other. Were they to do so, they could exchange only at world prices, as any party doing worse in a trade than the world price ratio could have recourse to the world market instead. In that case we lose nothing by neglecting trade between Arcadia and Bella in the initial state.

When Arcadia and Bella form a Kemp–Wan tariff-compensating customs union, what does this amount to? The simple answer is that it is equivalent to allowing the two trade ministries to trade with each other. Then, because trade with the outside world is frozen, it is no longer the case that they can exchange only at world prices. A necessary and sufficient condition for the two ministries to be able to trade gainfully on behalf of their residents is that they start with different relative prices. That is not the same as saying that they must start with different tariff rates. We saw that with the Viner example above. There, all three countries had the same tariff on wine imports, but that turned out to be consistent with different national prices ratios. In A the ratio was set by E's cost of wine in terms of bread plus the 25% tariff, giving a wine price of 1.25. In B and E, however, the wine price is set by the domestic cost of wine production, giving wine prices of 1.20 and 1.00 in B and E respectively.

When the two ministries trade with each other they must establish an exchange ratio at which neither wishes to trade more or less, and that in turn must be the same as the relative price that the goods will command on both auction markets. Yet with the exception of the odd case in which the two ministries between them import the joint imports of the two countries under free trade – but mal-distributed between the two – the final price ratio established will not be the world price ratio. Hence we end up with the trade ministries, now combined into one ministry, still auctioning off the same supply of imports, but now in a single auction for both countries.

The idea behind the tariff-compensating customs union is that it will harvest the advantages of trade creation between its members while avoiding trade diversion. No surprise then to discover that a tariff-compensating customs union will achieve nothing for a pure trade-diverting case, such as the basic Viner example above. Before the customs union is formed in that case, A is importing wine from E and B is producing its own wine. The tariff-compensating union must maintain the wine imports from E. In that case there is no gain from further trade between A and B. That is true only when bread and wine are consumed in fixed proportions. With the possibility of substitution in consumption it is no longer true that there can be no gain from making more wine from B available to A.

Lastly we come to the formal mathematical proof of the Kemp–Wan result. The theorem has force in the non-trivial case, when, on account of tariffs or other trade constraints, in place prior to the formation of the customs union, the initial state for A and B together is not Pareto efficient conditional on the sum of net trade flows from and to E.

Theorem 3.1 (Kemp–Wan): *A customs union can always be made world Pareto improving (strictly weakly Pareto improving) if the external tariff is adjusted so as to leave trade with the rest of the world unaffected by the formation of the customs union.*

Proof: Consider the redirection of the resources of combined A and B, plus changes in their productive activities and exchanges, always respecting the constraint that net trades with E shall not be altered.

This can at worse allow no Pareto improvement for the residents of A and B. Yet, as A and B have tariffs against each other in the initial situation, the presumption is that rearrangements involving only the activities of producers and consumers in A and B will allow a Pareto improvement on the original pre-union state of affairs. As trade with the outside is unchanged, it can take place at the same prices, and no outside interest is harmed. These constant trades with the outside world comprise constants, like the quantities of natural resources available to the economy. By the fundamental theorem of welfare economics, the Pareto-better state of affairs can be decentralised by a price system with lump-sum transfers between agents in the union, as required to ensure that all shall gain and none shall lose. The net trades with E will have equilibrium shadow prices, because, although they are fixed, we can imagine them being slightly different. Given these shadow prices, we have two sets of prices for traded goods in the customs union combined economy. The differences between these prices define optimal external tariff (or subsidy) rates for the customs union economy as part of a general equilibrium. QED

3.4 Problems with the Kemp–Wan result

If the Kemp–Wan theorem seems too neat to be true, notice some problems. First, it depends on the existence of lump-sum transfers, because the FTWE depends on assuming the use as necessary of the ideal theoretical type of income redistribution that has no effect on incentives: the lump-sum transfer. Lump-sum transfers are required to show that a Pareto-efficient state of the economy can be decentralised by a price system because the proof of the FTWE shows that a Pareto-efficient state of the economy can be supported by a price system and an appropriate set of lump-sum transfers. This price system has the property that producers producing the quantities designated by the equilibrium state, and using the inputs similarly detailed, would not find it more profitable to deviate from the equilibrium state. In just the same way, consumers consuming the quantities detailed by the equilibrium, and supplying labour as described, would not find it preferable to deviate from the equilibrium, assuming, of course, that any deviation must be a movement along the budget constraint defined by the equilibrium prices.

To summarise, we can take any efficient state and associate with it prices such that each agent will wish to stay with that efficient state when the possibilities of moving away from it are defined by those prices. So if we find an efficient state we can make it a price equilibrium. That price equilibrium will place each agent on a budget plane. For a consumer it defines minimum expenditure to attain a given level of utility. For a producer it defines maximum profit. In this exercise a consumer might in principle be placed on any budget plane. Yet in a standard competitive equilibrium each consumer has a natural budget plane: that one defined by the value of the resources owned by this same consumer, including the right to share in the profits of any firm in the ownership of which the consumer may participate. So to make any Pareto-efficient state an equilibrium, we have to be able to take any consumer on one budget plane and place him or her on another budget plane. Such a shift in budget plane can be thought of as a redistribution of initial resources, and, because it is arbitrary and independent of any decision by the consumer, it is called a lump-sum transfer.

Suitably chosen lump-sum transfers play an essential role in the Kemp–Wan theorem's demonstration that a customs union can always be made Pareto improving. That is no surprise when we consider that a tariff-compensating customs union is an attempt to harvest the benefits of more free trade (trade creation) while avoiding the inefficiencies associated with trade diversion. Yet we know that free trade is not Pareto improving as such. Not every type of individual can expect to gain from the increased general efficiency. Indeed, a loss to the owners of factors used intensively in highly protected sectors is quite typical. This is the classic Stolper–Samuelson result, derived more than half a century ago, which shows that it could be rational for labour to support the protection of labour-intensive production, despite the general inefficiency that would follow, because that protection would raise the wage rate of labour by more than the increase in any consumer cost-of-living index. Hence in requiring lump-sum transfers in order to show that a customs union can be generally beneficial, we are only replicating a feature of the more familiar efficiency of free trade argument.

Unfortunately for the present purpose, lump-sum transfers have lost favour in modern public finance theory, although trade theory is still riddled with the assumption that they exist and can be used. The reasons for their unpopularity among taxation theorists are not far to seek. To suppose that one can redistribute income between agents in the economy to establish any efficient state is to violate two rather solid principles that state that:

- Information is a scarce good, for which reason tax systems have to be simple and to rely on information that those subject to the taxation can be expected to provide.
- Because a system of taxes or transfers changes the incentives of economic agents, transfers typically cannot be based on any criteria (such as earned income or place of residence) that the agent can choose to influence. Yet any taxation based on formal legislation, and subject to litigation in a court of law, must nominate criteria independent of who is to pay the tax.

It seems then that lump-sum taxation is absolutely impossible. Probably the theorists who use it do not intend it seriously. Rather it is a way of examining the efficiency of economic arrangements while setting issues of income distribution aside. While there is a long tradition of proceeding that way, it is not at all clear that it makes any sense. An approach to efficiency that depends upon assuming the existence of an impractical taxation instrument can establish efficiency only in a highly rarefied sense.

We can conclude therefore that the Kemp–Wan demonstration of the Pareto optimality of a tariff-compensating customs union is more a demonstration of the efficiency of a well-designed customs union, according to quite an abstract definition of efficiency, than a practical scheme for implementing the formation of a customs union so that all will benefit. Yet even if we do not allow that to worry us, we should notice that the formation of a tariff-compensating customs union depends upon a complex adjustment of external tariff rates, which adjustment may be hard to calculate, and the implementation of which may breach GATT rules. It may be necessary, for instance, to raise some tariff rates in order to maintain a constant level of trade. The GATT, however, prohibits the increase of tariffs except under particular circumstances, and maintaining constant trade for a customs union is not one of them.

3.5 Tariff compensation combined with optimal indirect taxation

The way round the problem of the impracticality of lump-sum taxation is to look at an approach that does not use it. It is known that trade can often be shown to be gainful in the Pareto sense, to the benefit of all, without recourse to lump-sum transfers, if optimal indirect taxes are employed. This is the basis of the open economy interpretation of the Diamond–Mirrlees theorem.[5] The idea is that indirect tax changes could in principle protect consumers, whose welfare is at stake, from the price changes due to alterations in trade flows that must be allowed to affect production decisions. Could a similar idea be applied to customs union formation, and what would that mean? Before attempting to answer that question, we first review the Diamond–Mirrlees result.

To understand the method behind the theorem, consider what Pareto optimality entails. The usual definition is purely technical: an allocation is not Pareto efficient if the technical production possibilities of the economy would permit a reallocation that would be weakly preferred by all, and strongly preferred by at least one. More generally, Pareto efficiency can be defined relative to specific policy instruments. An example would be an allocation that cannot be improved on by any change in the taxes and feasible (e.g. non-lump-sum) instruments at the disposal of the authorities.

To find out what is Pareto optimal subject to the use of certain instruments we cannot proceed as the FTWE did. That is, we cannot take a Pareto-optimal state and show that competitive equilibrium prices are associated with it. The reason is that, once we move away from the purely technical definition of efficiency, prices become part of the feasibility requirements for a state of the economy, and the analysis has to take that into account. To this end, consider what determines the welfare of the individuals or groups who people an economy, including economies that we are going to merge into a customs union, and the world outside. The obvious answer would say that it is what they consume, the work they do, etc. In other words, consumption quantities in the broadest sense. Yet it is often more useful to look at welfare as dependent indirectly on the prices faced by agents, including wage rates.

For a complete specification we would have to add transfer incomes, such as dividends and government hand-outs, and quantity constraints, which would include an unemployed worker's inability to obtain employment at the going wage rate, or a milk quota, such as those administered by the EC or the Canadian government. Let us focus on prices as determinants of welfare, holding the other things constant, although they will not remain constant under the formation of a customs union.

Before looking at customs union formation, however, it helps to see how a Diamond–Mirrlees type of argument works out in the case of a standard gains-from-trade demonstration, such as those that figure prominently in basic international trade theory. As has already been noted, trade is gainful for everyone, even for a small undistorted economy, only if lump-sum transfers take care of possibly adverse income distribution effects. Gainful trade can hurt some parties, as is shown by the Stolper–Samuelson effect. Trade might lower the relative price of a good in the economy and this would harm the real income of the factor used intensively in the production of that good. If a tariff was previously holding the economy back from free trade, the precise welfare consequences depend on how the tariff revenue was spent previously. So let us assume that it was distributed neutrally, in which case the factor used intensively in producing the goods whose relative price has fallen will definitely suffer a welfare loss. This is no problem for the textbook trade theory, which assumes that lump-sum transfers will compensate any losers. Here we are not assuming that lump-sum transfers can be used, so we have to take the welfare loss seriously. Suppose, however, that trade offers gains in the efficiency of production, as is typically the case. To avoid harm to consumers, why not hold consumer prices constant? This is the idea that underlies the Diamond–Mirrlees theorem on the efficiency of public sector production. The mechanism for holding consumer prices constant is optimal indirect taxes and subsidies.

Again the references provided give the details essential for a mathematical demonstration of the theorem. Figure 3.3 shows how the theorem works. In the figure, *PP* is the production possibility curve for the country we are considering. World prices are shown by the slope of the tangent to *PP* at *A′*. Hence if producers faced world prices they would produce at *A′*. Initially, however, a tariff against the import of good 1 is in place and this moves the relative prices in the economy to the slope of the line that is a tangent to *PP* at *A*, which is where producers produce with the tariff in place. Then consumers too face the with-tariff relative prices and they consume at *B*, and the trade line is *AB*. The indifference curve of one consumer *II* is shown tangential to the price line at *B*. Note, however, that as consumers' relative prices will never alter, the preferences of any number of consumers aggregate perfectly to give non-intersecting community indifference curves. Hence the figure can be interpreted as depicting a one-consumer economy if the reader finds that easier, but that interpretation is not required.

To obtain the full benefits available from trade, producers are faced with world prices and production moves to *A′*. When tariffs are cut, precisely offsetting indirect taxes come into effect, which means that consumer prices are unchanged. It is as if when the tariff on the

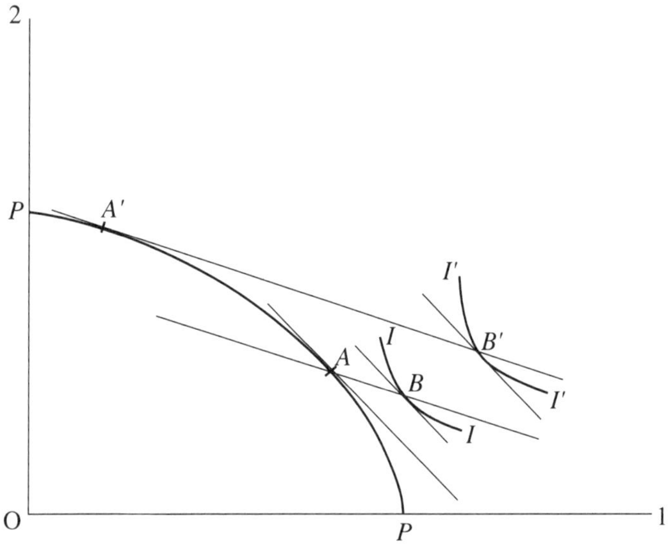

Figure 3.3

import of a car costing £10,000, including £2000 import duty, is cut to zero, a domestic sales tax on that same car of the same £2000 is imposed. With the new production having a higher value at world prices, consumers can enjoy a positive income effect, which is shown in the figure as the outward shift in the budget constraint that takes them from B to B' and to a higher utility level on $I'I'$. The income increase is effected by the government cutting all consumer taxes to maintain relative prices, which may involve it in subsidising some consumptions. In any case, the benefit from increased trade has been shown without any recourse to lump-sum taxes or transfers.

With such a powerful method established, it is obviously important to know whether it can be extended to the case in which the gains from trade involved are not the fuller opening of a small country to world markets, as shown in Figure 3.3, but are rather the trade-creating effects of a tariff-compensating customs union. As far as I know, the only place where this is done in print is in Dixit and Norman's textbook,[6] but even there the result receives less emphasis than it merits. The argument is a straightforward extension of the Diamond–Mirrlees proof.

There are two differences between the present argument and the open economy version of the Diamond–Mirrlees theorem, as illustrated in Figure 3.3. In that case there was only one country that reformed its internal equilibrium, and in doing so it changed (greatly increased, as it happened, in Figure 3.3) its trade with the outside world. Now we have at least two countries that form a customs union. Their reform is similar, in that the prices faced by consumers will be unchanged, but now net trades of all the reforming countries together with the outside world will be held constant, as in the Kemp–Wan theorem.

When one country is reformed, all the consumers initially face the same relative prices. So only one set of prices has to be sustained by the optimal indirect taxes. When several countries reform by forming a customs union, they must start with different relative prices, for otherwise there would be no scope for gain. Therefore optimum indirect taxes that ensure no harm to any consumers (no Stolper–Samuelson type of effect) must preserve more than one set of consumer prices. The means by which this is achieved is *country-specific optimum indirect taxation*. This gives us the final result of the present chapter:

Theorem 3.2 (Dixit–Norman): *A customs union can always be made (weakly) world Pareto improving, without the use of lump-sum transfers, if suitable tariffs and country-specific optimal indirect taxes are adopted in all member countries.*

3.6 Conclusions concerning customs union theory

Despite the wide range of results covered in this chapter, a broad summary is not too difficult. First, because a customs union may divert trade, it is not necessarily an innocuous institution. Our Viner example shows that the burden of trade diversion need not fall on the countries excluded from the union – although this is more likely to happen the larger is the union. Indeed, the same example shows that the burden may fall on the country that superficially seems to benefit, the one that obtains a lower domestic price for the good that it imports. The Viner theorem, however extended, establishes an approach to customs union theory in which the consequences of a union that holds its external tariffs, while allowing free trade between its members, are assessed.

More interesting for assessing the potential of the customs union is the tariff-compensating customs union, which adjusts its common external tariff to hold trade with the rest of the world constant. This was Ohyama's idea and Kemp and Wan showed that a tariff-compensating customs union can always be world Pareto improving. These authors made use of standard textbook lump-sum taxes. The use of these always tends to trivialise problems of income distribution. Yet an extension of the Diamond–Mirrlees theorem shows that a customs union that exploits the full potential of optimal indirect taxation does not need to employ anything as fantastic as lump-sum taxes to gain the benefits of trade creation while avoiding both harm to the outside world and adverse effects on domestic income distribution. It will however need country-specific indirect taxation[7].

We seem to be moving to the conclusion that customs union design is everything. By extension the same point would seem to apply to trading blocks. There is something in this, and certainly there can be good and bad customs unions, as there can be good and bad trading blocks. Yet there are some further technical problems to take into account, and these are examined in the next chapter.

Appendix: Tariff averaging

This appendix makes use of the following mathematical result, which is stated in many textbooks of mathematical analysis but is proved here because the proof is exceptionally easy, and seeing it demonstrated makes clear the exact nature of the result.

Theorem 3.3 (generalised mean-value theorem): *Let $f(x)$ be a scalar-valued continuously differentiable function of x in R^n, and let $F(x)$ be the Jacobian matrix of partial derivatives of $f(.)$ evaluated at x. Then for all x^1 and x^2, there is a scalar value λ $(0 \leq \lambda \leq 1)$ such that:*

$$f(x^2) - f(x^1) = F[\lambda x^2 + (1 - \lambda)x^1].(x^2 - x^1) \tag{3.6}$$

Proof: Define $g(\lambda)$ as:

$$g(\lambda) = f[\lambda x^2 + (1 - \lambda)x^1] \tag{3.7}$$

Then $g(1) = f(x^2)$; $g(0) = f(x^1)$; and:

$$f(x^2) - f(x^1) = g(1) - g(0) \tag{3.8}$$

By the standard mean value theorem, there exists a value of λ on [0,1], such that:

$$g(1) - g(0) = g'(\lambda); \tag{3.9}$$

where $g'(\ )$ is the first derivative of $g(\ )$. However,

$$g'(\lambda) = F[\lambda x^2 + (1-\lambda)x^1].(x^2 - x^1) \tag{3.10}$$

as required.

What is notable about the theorem is that it shows that the lying between property of the mean value point in the standard result generalises in a many dimensional space to lying between in the sense of being a convex combination.

Now consider N countries that form a customs union. Initially they all have their own tariffs shown by vectors t^i ($i = 1, \ldots, N$). The vector of excess demand of country i is $x^i(p^0 + t^i)$, where p^0 is the prior-to-tariffs prices common to all countries in a world general equilibrium. Before the customs union is formed, the summed excess demands of all the N producers – their net trade with the outside world – is:

$$\hat{x}(p^0; t^1, t^2, ..., t^N) = \sum_{i=1}^{N} x^i(p^0 + t^i) \tag{3.11}$$

If a trade-neutral common external tariff is defined as the tariff that makes the net trade with the outside world the same as it is with the various tariffs in effect prior to the formation of the union, and if that tariff vector is denoted t^0, then t^0 satisfies:

$$\hat{x}(p^0; t^1, t^2, ..., t^N) = \hat{x}(p^0; t^0, t^0, ..., t^0); \tag{3.12}$$

which is:

$$\sum_{i=1}^{N} x^i(p^0 + t^i) = \sum_{i=1}^{N} x^i(p^0 + t^0) \tag{3.13}$$

Equation (3.13) is not only valid for a small union, the formation of which does not affect its terms of trade. This is because p^0 is the terms of trade with the rest of the world, however large or small, and as trade with that rest of the world will not be affected, the customs union is like a small country, even if it is large. Now let there be m goods, and let X^i be the matrix of partial derivatives of the excess demand function of country i, defined as:

$$X^i = \begin{bmatrix} \frac{\partial x_1^i}{\partial p_1} & \frac{\partial x_1^i}{\partial p_2} & \cdot & \frac{\partial x_1^i}{\partial p_m} \\ \frac{\partial x_2^i}{\partial p_1} & \frac{\partial x_2^i}{\partial p_2} & \cdot & \frac{\partial x_2^i}{\partial p_m} \\ \cdot & \cdot & \cdot & \cdot \\ \frac{\partial x_m^i}{\partial p_1} & \cdot & \cdot & \frac{\partial x_m^i}{\partial p_m} \end{bmatrix} \tag{3.14}$$

Obviously X^i is a function of $p^0 + t^i$. Taking the difference between the right- and left-hand sides of the equation and applying the generalised mean value theorem, we obtain:

$$\sum_{i=1}^{N} X^{i*}.(t^0 - t^i) = 0 \tag{3.15}$$

where X^{i*} is X^i evaluated at $p^0 + t^{i*}$; with t^{i*} chosen to satisfy the requirement of the generalised mean value theorem. From the last equation we obtain:

$$\left[\sum_{i=1}^{N} X^{i*}\right].t^0 = \sum_{i=1}^{N} X^{i*}.t^i \tag{3.16}$$

From which:

$$t^0 = \left[\sum_{i=1}^{N} X^{i*}\right]^{-1}.\left\{\sum_{i=1}^{N} X^{i*}.t^i\right\} \tag{3.17}$$

It will be seen that the union-neutral tariff vector is a linear transform of a sum of linear transforms of the initial individual country tariff vectors. That is not tariff averaging as tariff averaging would normally be understood. First, the computed tariff vector is weighted averaging if it is tariff averaging, because tariffs are multiplied by terms that are slopes of demand functions evaluated at points defined by the generalised mean value theorem, which means evaluated at a convex combination of initial and final tariffs. That should not concern us, because weighted averaging is a form of averaging. Indeed, the presence of slopes of demand functions in the formula is reassuring, because they take care of the size of country anomaly with strict arithmetic averaging, which was mentioned above. Yet equation (3.17) for t^0 is not weighted tariff averaging in the sense that tariffs for individual goods are averaged across countries, not even with weighting, as we might allow if we extended the EC rule somewhat. The point is that, ignoring the possibility of zeros in the matrix inverse $[\sum_{i=1}^{N} X^{i*}]^{-1}$, changing the rate of tariff on any good in any country changes every component of t^0 – changes the rate of tariff on every good.

To interpret the tariff averaging rule as an attempt to avoid any change in trade between a customs union and the rest of the world, and then to convict a simple arithmetic average of national individual-good tariff rates for its failure to achieve that objective, may be to miss the point. Tariff averaging was not dreamed up by economists. At the time the theory of protection was in a primitive state, and the Treaty of Rome does not embody any particular theory of protection. Its authors felt that averaging tariffs would about balance out. They were not correct in this view. Yet if the matrix inverse $[\sum_{i=1}^{N} X^{i*}]^{-1}$ should be effectively diagonal, in the sense that setting its off-diagonal terms to zero makes a negligible difference, or provides an acceptable approximation, then the exact formula for the neutral common tariff reduces to weighted tariff averaging.

Notes

1 Aside from the issue of whether arithmetic tariff averaging holds external protection of the union constant, of which more below, it should be noted that the EC, by allocating the sum of existing import quotas to the whole union, in effect increased protection because countries not quota restricted became quota restricted.
2 Corden (1984, section 11) provides a survey. See also Dixit and Norman (1980) and Jovanavić (1992).
3 Balassa (1975) argues that trade creation predominated over trade diversion for the EC for trade in industrial goods.
4 See Varian (1984), pp. 200–1.
5 See Diamond and Mirrlees (1971) and Dasgupta and Stiglitz (1974).
6 See Dixit and Norman (1980), pp. 191–5.
7 On the determination and administration of indirect taxes in the EC, see Smith (1993).

CHAPTER 4

Policy instruments and block design

4.1 Producer interests and job opportunities

The several results of Chapter 3 may seem too neat to be true. The almost perfect customs union is achievable by means of relatively simple, if precisely tuned, instruments. Of course there are many problems. First, the argument neglects the important influence of the producer interest on welfare. Specifically, profit or rents do not enter into private welfare functions. Secondly, employment opportunities are unimportant; only the wage rates at which various kinds of employment are on offer matter. These are important considerations, yet in theory some of them could be covered quite effectively by extending the devices available to the authorities beyond the limited set of tariffs and indirect taxes. If, for example, customs unification makes the employment-rationing constraint for a particular type of labour more severe, governments could employ more of that type of labour to conserve labour demand.

In principle what can be achieved is limited mainly by the ingenuity of the theorist, or policy designer. Yet there must be limits. The second best is the second best, and nothing will ever be as good as lump-sum transfers. The major consideration is different, however. The most serious problems have to do with information and incentives.

Note the various components of the argument and how they contribute to the way the reform works. Producer prices are equalised throughout the union. The common external tariff is adjusted so that external trade is constant (and hence at constant prices). Consumer prices are changed inside each country but in such a way that everyone benefits. They are not equalised across countries because country-specific indirect taxes are part of the solution. Notice in particular that goods and services are distinguished only by sign in the formal mathematical version of the result (which has not been presented but which follows exactly the form of the diagrammatic argument). Hence country-specific indirect taxes include country-specific factor subsidies or taxes. For this reason it might be helpful to refer to household prices.

This last point answers one puzzle but highlights a problem at the same time. Most readers will feel instinctively that the nation-specific interests that are threatened by free trade among a block of nations will predominantly be producer interests not consumer interests, where producer interests are taken to include the individuals as workers or profit sharers. Consumers as consumers, this argument would say, usually benefit unambiguously from free trade, which tends to give them cheaper goods and more competition. The use of the Viner model has illustrated this proposition. The direct effects of the union in the example were beneficial to consumers (cheaper goods prices), although the trade-diverting production effects added up to a net loss for consumers in one country. We have not yet examined non-competitive models and increasing returns and these can introduce important qualifications, but the conclusion mainly stands.

On balance it is right to think that conflicting producer interests, including the interests of employees in specific activities, pose the biggest problems for free intra-block trade if it is required to be for the benefit of everyone, and one could argue that a model of common external tariff adjustment and optimal nation-specific indirect taxes trivialises those problems. If this is correct, it should be possible to point out where the model sneaks a rabbit into the hat, and it is clear where this is done.

By assuming that households can be fully protected from the costs of a change in production structure by operating on household prices (including wage rates) the model assumes that household welfare does not depend on what values producer prices take and on what production activities are. Among the various reasons why this might not be the case, two are of outstanding significance. First, producer prices determine profits, particularly, and more generally rents of various kinds, which share in common the feature that they cannot be identified with the sale or purchase of a specific good or service to which a tax or subsidy can be attached. Secondly, the model is constructed on the basis of the standard competitive equilibrium model, in which prices are what matter and quantity constraints play no role. This is terribly unrealistic. Imagine workers employed in an inefficient steel sector about to be pitched into a customs union. 'Do not worry,' says their government, 'our policy will protect your wage rates.' 'Thank you,' say the workers, 'now what about our jobs?'

The two points are really the same. The value of an employment opportunity is an instance of a rent. Where wages and prices are perfectly flexible, as in the competitive model, most of this rent disappears. Some persists, because there are such things as adjustment costs, which include real costs, not just laziness and conservatism. A case in point would be costs of retraining and moving. If we pursue these issues we soon get into questions that may be called administrative, although that term should not be taken in any sense to belittle them, for they are most important.

Take two examples. On the negative side, the Dixit–Norman theorem shows that a customs union can be weakly Pareto improving for the world as a whole and for each participating country if we allow external tariff adjustment and country-specific indirect taxation. Country-specific indirect taxation poses no problem for a customs union but is inconsistent with a common market. A common market allows free mobility of goods and factors within the union, so that customs posts become redundant. It is striking to note that the institution that is popularly known as the European Common Market has never been a common market since its original foundation with the Treaty of Rome. Only recently has the Community, currently of 12 members, become a genuine common market via the radical and far-reaching single market exercise, largely completed in January 1993, although further detailed implementation with regard to labour mobility and other matters progresses slowly. Thus the conclusion is that there exist potentially useful administrative devices of which we could in principle make use in a customs union, but which we cannot employ in a single market.

Against this point the advocates of the single market exercise, notably the EC Commission itself, argue that a common market permits easier and less costly exchange than does a customs union. How much is this worth? Some estimates of substantial gains have been announced.[1] These are frankly guesstimates and it is hardly possible to know the answer in advance, or ever to know with any precision. The econometric task of extracting the effects of the European single market from everything else that will affect Europe's development over the next five years will no doubt prove to be as indefinite as such exercises usually do. A sceptic would say that Europe has already gained most of the large benefits of economic integration and that a single market for lorries will add a little bit extra but not huge gains.

On a less pessimistic note, consider a second point. The Dixit–Norman argument shows what nice things can be done with optimally designed indirect taxes. We can do more of course with additional instruments. It has been remarked how changes in rents are an awkward aspect of reform where the aim is to make everyone benefit. So why not compensate those whose rents are reduced by reform? That would include financial compensation for loss of employment, but, better still, why not provide employment for those who become involuntarily unemployed as a result of reform? Best of all, why not go all the way and adopt the lump-sum compensations and levies of classical welfare economics? Then all we have to worry about is that our reforms should promote general efficiency, and we can always cut the cake up in such a way that we will achieve all-round benefit. Can we indeed?

Not really. The problems under three headings are: information, rent-seeking and time-consistency.[2] Information points us to the consideration that reforms have to be computationally and administratively feasible. Elaborate compensation schemes requiring full and precise information of the general equilibrium outcome are not administratively feasible, and even if that information were available it would have to be available in such a way that it would be proof against dispute and legal argument. In opposition to legal requirements, lump-sum transfers have to be addressed to individuals by name; they cannot be derived from known formulae of which agents would be aware and to which they would react in their maximising behaviour. An instance of this would be income taxation affecting the supply of labour. Distortions arise and transfers are not costless.

Rent-seeking takes this process one step further and adds additional resource costs. Knowing that formulae will be applied to the calculation of compensation payments, agents will expend valuable resources, such as lobbying time, to try and influence what these formulae will be. The standard rent-seeking model point, as originally made by Bhagwati, Krueger and others,[3] says that the distortionary costs of tariff protection exceed the excess burden of the tariffs as such (often small for modest tariffs) because we have to add in the resource diversion that arises when agents try to divert the rents that tariffs provide towards themselves. The point, however, is more general. Administrative edict always creates and destroys rents. Then rational agents apply resources in the attempt to influence how that administration will affect their interests. This effort costs real resources. Its effects one may or may not like, but even if, fortuitously, the nice guys win in the competition, the activity itself remains wasteful.

The time-consistency problem is encountered when we note that the effects of reform last through time and agents plan and react to reform through time. That makes the problem of information especially acute, but set that issue aside for the time being, and focus on problems of paying for losses and compensations when these work themselves out through time. With full information, time seems to add no essential new principle. The appropriate payments should be calculated and made once-and-for-all, and they should represent minimum costs of adjusting to reform.

The point may be illustrated by considering a region within a trade block – imagine a not-well-off region that housed some inefficient and highly protected activities. With union, a great deal of unemployment is created by the efficient reallocation of community-wide resources. Suppose, for the sake of discussion, that much of this labour should either migrate or retrain and that funds have been made available to pay the minimum costs to the labour force of doing that. An alternative would be to subsidise investment in activities that would re-employ the labour in the same place with the same skills. This would be inefficient but attractive to the workers concerned. They lost the argument, however, and have been given money instead.

Suppose that the money comes to a local authority with the idea that it should be spent on migration assistance and retraining, but there is some fungibility. Imagine that the authority can divert some of the funds to other purposes. If the compensation funding had been an entirely mechanical process run by a machine that just calculates the right payments for Pareto optimality and then self-destructs, it might not be a good idea for the local authority to divert funds in the manner described. But in fact compensation payments are not made by soulless machines, they are made by institutions, staffed by human beings with values and objectives, including the welfare of others, or at very least a wish to avoid political embarrassment arising from the condition of individuals and regions. The central authority might know or suspect that the diversion of funding has taken place. Now it is presented with a situation in which the case for funding that persuaded it to fund at the previous stage still confronts it. Morally it ought perhaps to say to the local authority: you wasted the funds, so that is that, not a penny more. Can it really do that? Could it credibly threaten to do that, as it would like to be able to do?

Put simply, the point is that standard welfare economics disembodies the process of transfer and compensation, as though this could be undertaken by an uninvolved agent. A fully informed agent, certainly, but it is not only the information assumption that is decidedly odd. It is even more the absurdly depersonalised mechanical way in which the whole process is supposed to operate that defies belief. Conscious value-bearing agents are bound by the requirement that they behave rationally, and a refusal to pay further compensation in the second period is impossible. It is not time consistent, not a sub-game perfect strategy in the language of game theory. Knowing this, the local authority can divert some of the funding knowing that more will be paid.

Why should we bother with ingenious and troublesome arguments about the design and internal administration of the model non-trade-diverting customs union? Why not go straight to the best of the best – to the global free trade equilibrium? In the models used to demonstrate customs union theory – including neutral unions – free trade is nearly always best. On the test of revealed preference it seems that free trade is far from being best; it is indeed so painful and unattractive that governments take a lot of trouble to avoid it.

This type of observation has spawned a literature on the political economy of protection, including an elaborate model of political economic general equilibrium, with voters imperfectly informed to the optimal extent, and even black hole tariffs that extinguish trade altogether.[4] It is doubtful whether economists do well to get too street wise where protectionism is concerned. Our comparative advantage lies in illuminating the real gains to be had from more liberal trade and taking into account the weighty considerations of distortions, externalities and income distribution, problems for which protection is better than no policy, but is far from being a good policy response.

Results already discussed allow us to counter what might be called second-bestism. A should protect because B is protecting, to avoid the distortion that would arise if A liberalised alone. Every distortion justifies a similar distortion: think of an optimum tariff answered by a maximising optimal tariff response. The popular version of second-bestism is the so-called level playing field argument, which says that free trade is fine in principle, but only with the proviso that no country is doing anything to distort world trade. We have seen how partial reform can be effective, so it is no surprise that second-bestism must be questioned. Yet where trade reform is politically or economically painful, trade reform must become to some extent an international bargaining game.

Given any particular reason why governments interfere with free trade, we will often find that this consideration importantly affects the consequence of customs union formation. Take a self-sufficiency objective, a dislike of trade with outsiders or a preference for trade with insiders. Not a particularly admirable motive, you may think, but an important one. How this is affected by customs union formation depends on the precise definition of the motive. Does national self-sufficiency translate to a union self-sufficiency objective?

After customs union formation, people, presumably, and in any case governments, are meant to exclude chauvinistic feelings towards their new partners. Whether or not they do so, a customs union affects both the need for chauvinistic objectives and the costs of meeting such objectives where they persist. Suppose, to illustrate the point, that Europeans do not like to be dependent on foreign food supplies.[5] That is a taste that comes expensive for the European countries with a relatively poor comparative advantage in some kinds of agricultural production, such as the cultivation of winter vegetables. If European countries combine and merge their agricultures, including southern countries with a better comparative advantage in the agriculture concerned, and if chauvinistic feelings concerning agricultural trade are translated to the additional EC members, then the objective may be less costly and trade distorting than it would be if pursued by individual countries on a go-it-alone basis.

A neat story, but hardly a recognisable description of the Common Agricultural Policy, though to note the differences is illuminating. The CAP has created self-sufficiency, if not Community surplus, for many agricultural products, some, such as oil seeds, depending on heavy subsidies. Yet it was not mainly as a self-sufficiency-promoting device that it came into being. Rather, income transfer, from consumers in general to farmers in particular, was the leading and undisguised objective. From richer North European consumers to farmers who were often French, one might add. The French are no more self-serving than any other nation, but they happened to enjoy the influence at the inception of the Community to establish a system of agricultural protection very similar to the one employed in France. The expansion of the EC and trends in agro-technology have made the CAP notoriously expensive and inefficient, and the dumping of surpluses to which it gave rise translated its inherent inefficiencies to world-wide agricultural markets, and generated provocation to US agricultural interests, which is one of the facts of current trade diplomacy.

It is not uncommon to find that protection exports adjustment problems outside the area in which protection is applied. What is interesting for the present discussion is that the objectives of the CAP have not transcended national and local objectives and criteria. Thus Germany, which should, on simple political economic grounds, be a critic of the policy, has seen its general policy captured on one occasion at least by the Bavarian farm lobby. This is only a familiar type of case often argued by analysts of protection. Protection creates interest groups regardless of how inappropriate that protection may have been initially to the whole nation in which the interest group finds itself.

Agricultural protection might be a case of the curiously titled non-economic objectives. These are typically taken to be binding constraints on the economic outcome which can enter a public valuation function only lexicographically, bypassing questions of trade-offs. The term is often applied sloppily. For example, food security is said to be a non-economic objective, presumably because in the model we actually examine no value attached to food security. Yet that only makes our model partial, not food security a non-economic objective. The term non-economic serves to protect the objective from critical examination and that may account for its popularity. Alan Winters has shown that economic analysis can be applied very effectively to the question of whether agricultural protection makes an important contribution to food security, with very unfavourable conclusions for the idea.[6] Non-economic objectives are a reason for tariffs only when other instruments such as subsidies are ruled out.[7] An exception to this proposition is encountered when the non-economic objective concerns trade as such (e.g. a self-sufficiency objective); however, in practice this is indistinguishable from chauvinism.

If Chapter 3 was the chapter of the perfect result, the present chapter is an essay in the art of the possible. The Kemp–Wan theorem constructs the ideal customs union on the foundation of lump-sum transfers. It is easy to show that only lump-sum transfers will do and some of the distortions entailed by non-lump-sum transfers have already been noted. Yet the Kemp–Wan result underlines the fact that transfers and compensations may be vital if a customs union is not to be divisive. It is true that ideal indirect taxes, including factor taxes or subsidies, can do the same job, although not as well. Yet we have seen that there are many problems in applying that result.

Such considerations suggest that we should look at transfers and compensation as imperfect but essential instruments for the effective customs union, recognising that this will be the examination of the far-from-perfect intervention, rather than of theorems on supporting Pareto optimality. Even if no system of transfers and compensation is perfect, some are surely worse than others, and that indicates that establishing some principles will be worthwhile.

The EC has adopted the principle that funding shall be made available to promote the economic convergence of poorer regions towards the Community average. The CAP was motivated by a wish to bring the incomes of farmers up to the general level. Generally, however, EC initiatives under the disbursement of structural, cohesion and social funds have taken the form of regional policy that targets particularly infrastructure and labour retraining. It is not difficult to extract the philosophy that underlies the design and employment of these instruments. The market system and labour mobility are assumed to be capable of taking care of regional disparities. The funding oils the wheels and assists the required transfer of resources. I have already criticised this philosophy on the grounds that redistribution and adjustment subsidy are not at all the same thing, with the implication that both may be required.[8] That argument is correct from the analytical point of view, but one must also recognise, as was conceded, that theoretical misdirection may coincide with some important self-policing features. The EC could never afford to make funding available to unfortunate regions or interest groups on a need-the-money basis. The demands would be vast, the information needed to filter applications would never be obtainable, and the induced rent-seeking would involve a heavy cost in resource misallocation.

By tying funding to narrower 'adjustment assistance' expenditures, the system is made self-policing to some extent. Requiring that old fishing boats should be taken out of use as a condition for receiving grants to aid regions hit by the depletion of fish stocks helps with the over-fishing problem, ensures that only fishermen genuinely suffering economic hardship get the aid, and should stop the worst form of rent-seeking when fishing boats are built or maintained to catch subsidies instead of fish. The example is educational: the fisheries policy of the EC departs from it in some crucial respects, and has encountered serious problems directly as a consequence. Requiring fishing boats to stay in port for a certain number of days a year looks nearly the same as decommissioning fishing boats. In practice, however, that case is very different, and the reason is *agency*. Member governments administer the policy and some of these are tempted to free-ride, which in this context means claiming subsidies from the EC while laxly administering boat use regulation. That type of difficulty has notoriously plagued EC fisheries policy.

The problem is quite general and is one to which theoretical models that design optimal rules for customs unions are too easily blind. Current arguments concerning NAFTA often reflect the same type of issue. The US critics of NAFTA do not just claim that trade will be diverted to Mexico because of low labour costs, although they do assert that. They also argue that trade will be diverted because Mexico's administration of environmental and safety regulations will be slack. Moreover, these critics will often assert, for cultural and historical reasons, Mexico's administration of environmental and safety regulations cannot be other than slack.

One can easily turn this argument into a more general discussion of optimal customs union design. How diverse should the ideal customs union be? The Viner approach, which, notice, focuses on world efficiency, and hence not directly on the interests of customs union members, would say that diversity, while it offers valuable gains from trade creation, carries with it the danger of trade diversion. Yet a selfish customs union might like diversity for its trade-creating potential, and care little for adverse effects on the rest of the world. That is not equivalent to not minding about trade diversion, as we have seen, because trade diversion can harm customs union members. Even supposing this not to be the case, and that diversity provides large trade-creation benefits, diversity may bring with it political and administrative difficulties springing from income inequality and the manipulation of administrative practices for regional advantage. The extent to which these problems matter will depend in part on how far the customs union pursues economic convergence as an objective (as the EC is constitutionally required to do) or whether it cares less about that objective. Philosophers of European union will argue that political cohesion is important for successful economic and administrative cohesion.

Regardless of whether that is true, the fact remains that convergence of the European regions has been slow. This is in part because labour mobility, a topic that is addressed in the next chapter, is low. Another reason is that EC regional policy has not had much discernible effect on regional convergence. It shares this feature with national regional policies, which, when temporary and diversionary effects are taken out, have also proved to be unimpressive.

The customs union was seen by the GATT as a movement in the direction of free trade. The diverse customs union may fail in that regard in two respects. First, by producing trade diversion, it may move away from the ideal allocation defined by world free trade. Also, if its diversity generates internal tensions and inequalities, these may be exported to some extent via the external policy of the union. We have examined the non-trade-diverting union as an ideal, but that does not guarantee that it will be a political objective. Indeed, surely internal tensions in Western Europe, partly produced by macroeconomic difficulties, are what account for its trade unfriendliness to the newly opened-up economies of Eastern Europe. What is the general lesson here for the trade block? It may be that it is crucial in this context to see the trade block not only as a set of trading arrangements but also as an administrative unit. Our economic arguments have shown that block formation does not have to be harmful to the rest of the world. That is not to say that the block may not prove to be harmful for reasons of administration, because it colours maps in certain ways and defines bureaucratic responsibility and accountability in terms of insiders and outsiders.

Notes

1 See Emerson et al. (1988). For a more sceptical view, see Flam (1992).
2 See Bliss in Bliss and de Macedo (1990), pp. 18–55.
3 See Krueger (1974 and 1984).
4 See Magee, Brock and Young (1989).
5 If food security is the reason, agricultural protection, as it happens, is a poor means of achieving the objective. See Winters (1991b).
6 See Winters (1991b).
7 See Corden (1974), pp. 16–17.
8 See Bliss, Chapter 2 in Bliss and de Macedo, eds (1990).

CHAPTER 5

Trade blocks and migration

5.1 Modelling labour migration

In Chapters 3 and 4 above we have considered the trading block in terms of the Kemp–Ohyama–Wan model of a neutral non-trade-diverting union. It is a good model, getting directly to the heart of some of the most important issues. Yet it is an unrealistic model in many ways. It is constructed on the basis of the perfect competitive general equilibrium model, and some of the most important issues we need to work into the model flow directly from various aspects of reality that the competitive equilibrium model excludes or neglects. These include imperfect competition, of course, a topic that is addressed in Chapter 6. Another topic of great importance to the trade block and how it operates is migration. We will focus on the migration of labour first and add in a brief consideration of capital mobility later.

Migration is not obviously inconsistent with the competitive model, although the model needs to be clarified for application in that context. Note that the Arrow–Debreu model of general competitive equilibrium does not include any explicit indication of where agents live. Powerful clues, however, are provided by the bundle of goods that an agent chooses to consume, and the natural complementarities between them that we might associate with location in space. This agent owns a house in Brighton and buys groceries for delivery in Brighton; she lives in Brighton. But she sells labour for delivery in London; she must be a commuter. Similar arguments apply with the firm.

A more precise and unambiguous way of placing the economic agent in space is to specify one or more significant variables in the consumption set. For example, the consumption set of a Brighton agent might require the consumption of some kind of Brighton residential service (if only free-good sleeping space on a Brighton park bench). The trouble with that method is obvious. We do not want to specify agents' positions in space in such a way that we tie them down to living in one place when they could in fact migrate. When the powers of both consumption set and preferences are combined, however, a good representation of most situations should prove possible. Then her consumption set will allow our agent to move to Aberdeen should she so please; when a time budget will not allow her to commute daily to London, and if living in Aberdeen is not to her taste, the Aberdeen goods that her consumption set will force her to consume will rank below Brighton consumption.

So far, so good, but it would be wrong to suggest that migration can be taken care of fully by reinterpreting the competitive general equilibrium model. First, non-convexities play a very important role in spatial economics and hence in migration decisions.[1] Secondly, increasing returns to scale are very important where location is concerned.[2] The modern city in all its horrors is a great attractor of in-migration, yet it would not exist but for strongly increasing returns. Otherwise the bidding up of prices, including the price of building land, and major external diseconomies would drive cities out of business. People keep prophesying that this is about to happen; that we will soon all be working from home in the suburbs, etc. Yet this state of affairs is very slow to arrive, and the reason it does not happen is the economies of scale that the city provides.

Labour migration is a consumption decision. It is the choice of a point in the consumption set, from which position in space can be deduced. Under the usual assumptions of perfect competitive markets, complete information and no missing markets, market equilibrium is efficient. In the case of migration decisions, we cannot hope to draw on such results of standard general equilibrium theory. We have seen that non-convexities are fundamental to decisions concerning location in space. That implies that even existence of equilibrium might well be a problem. Yet, even if we ignore that issue, the outcome of free migration decisions, uninfluenced by policy interventions, is likely to be non-optimal.

Another way of placing migration within more general theoretical models is to note its connection with externalities. Increasing returns already entail externalities, because the individual agent adds or subtracts scale, hence giving or taking away benefits to other agents. Migration also involves straightforward external economies or diseconomies, often associated with diminishing returns. Migrants who move to a city may add to congestion and transport delays, imposing an external diseconomy on existing residents of that city. Equally the same migrant might just tip the balance in favour of constructing a bridge, hence reducing travel times for existing residents. In either case an externality is involved.

A bridge is a case of a public good, and the relation between migration and the provision of local public goods is the topic analysed by the famous Tiebout model.[3] That model, however, is unsuitable for the analysis of the particular case of a bridge and the critical population size needed to justify its construction. For that example plainly involves the increasing returns to scale implied by a great indivisibility. Tiebout argued that competition between different localities would provide mobile agents with a choice of public good menus. That would lead to a Pareto-optimal outcome because any Pareto improvement would define a group of agents and a new jurisdiction, the formation of which would implement the improvement directly. Obviously that argument does not work with increasing returns, or with any kind of externality. For then the withdrawal from one local public good regime to another may provide those who move with gains at the expense of others, and there will be no Pareto optimality.

These complex considerations and counter-considerations regarding migration are reflected in ambiguities on the part of policy makers. Thus the EC embodies the free movement of labour and capital in its founding treaty.[4] Yet it was not supposed that the free movement of factors would alone solve the problems of inequality and resource misallocation across the Community. Hence the active role given to the Commission in funding adjustment and convergence.[5] However, the connection between the funding of adjustment, and especially the funding of training, and labour mobility or migration is subtle. To enjoy the convenience of a general term, call all such funding *transfers*. Transfers may either encourage or inhibit labour mobility. If they provide jobs in a disadvantaged region, it is likely that out-migration will be discouraged. On the other hand, training in skills in higher demand, and more generously remunerated, outside the region is likely to encourage out-migration. Ireland illustrates the point tragically, both North and South of the border: by combining high educational standards with poor performance in job generation, it makes itself the European country with the highest level of net emigration.

5.2 Trade and migration as substitutes

In orthodox trade theory, trade in goods substitutes for the migration of factors.[6] These results are derived in a framework of constant returns to scale and perfect competition. The most powerful result of this type is the factor price equalization theorem, which states specific, but surprisingly weak, conditions under which trade will do all the work of bringing factor prices in different countries together, making labour migration for economic reasons redundant. The model in which this type of result can be derived is known as the the Heckscher–Ohlin model.[7]

Yet the idea that trade might be a substitute for migration is not only valid under constant returns. The simple idea of giving market access to exports so that unwelcome immigrants will not need to come can be understood by the most simple-minded politician. Such thinking is an element at least in the development of the concept of more formally organized free trade between the United States and Mexico, which finds its fullest expression in the plans for a NAFTA. The lack of an effective control of illegal migration across the Mexico/US frontier has long caused anxiety among those who are anxious about it. An influential argument held that the only way to stop the Mexicans coming was to improve their situation at home by giving them opportunities to export goods into the USA. Similar arguments have been heard applied to Europe and the Mahgreb countries of North Africa.

There will always be some truth in the idea that trade can substitute for factor migration, and there are instances where that model fits the facts perfectly. Ironically, some of these are cases in which a lack of trade, because of tariff or quota restrictions, has generated immigration. This seems to have happened in the UK fibre industry, where even protection did not enable producers to pay wages that would attract domestic labour, and the protected sector ended up employing immigrants, many from countries whose fibre exports caused the problem in the first place.

In general, however, the idea that trade and migration are complete substitutes does not survive the introduction of increasing returns and problems of imperfect information. It does not even survive allowing techniques of production to differ between different countries and regions. We take the last point first, because elucidating the relationship between differences in production functions, on the one hand, and scale and externality effects, on the other, importantly needs doing. A simple justification for the Heckscher–Ohlin assumption that possible techniques of production (production functions) are the same in all countries is that knowledge must be internationally mobile. If a new technique for machining car parts is developed in one country, there may be a period during which its transfer to other countries has not been effected; but in the modern world such periods are short and are getting shorter. In particular, patents are seldom an effective inhibition to the movement of technology. The firm that develops a new technique can readily license its use or set up a manufacturing subsidiary abroad.

Notwithstanding this point, it remains the case that substantial differences in productivity between different countries do persist. They exist even when the same good is produced, and even when the same multinational company owns the process. Why? One leading reason is scale. Very often the low-productivity country will be seen to be, on examination, the small country (small in terms of economic activity). Another reason has to do with the general efficiency of the economic environment, including how well the infrastructure operates, and how effectively different producers, or different production teams, within one firm cooperate. This varies greatly from country to country.

Thus a leading force driving labour migration is the pull of the productive high-wage region. The movement of labour is costly, and most long-distance labour migration has been towards areas that are already crowded. That is true at least for economic migration with an employment objective. In countries with well-off independent retired populations, the movement of the elderly has often been in the opposite direction. Thus, in the USA, this type of migration played a large role in the growth of Florida. Once an area grows, of course, the young will follow to serve the needs of the elderly. Also, Florida has attracted manufacturing and service activities that can locate where they please, especially activities with low-volume material inputs, high-tech and high value added. Some of even this is a scale effect, because even the footloose industry does not locate where the infrastructure and complementary activities have not developed.

Scale and complementaries between neighbouring activities account for the fact that capital frequently does not move to the labour. Such arguments amount to refinements of the basic Heckscher–Ohlin approach, which has production locating where unit costs are minimal. Adding scale and costs not directly attributable to purchased inputs extends and clarifies this theory. One can take this type of argument further and look at the implications for the location of economic activity, and hence of the forces pulling labour movement, of tax legislation and economic regulation. Examples of this type of effect include: wage and employment laws, environmental and safety rules, competition and regulation regimes, and all the paraphernalia of the modern state's control of and influence on economic activity.

Most of these last influences will have their largest impact on decisions concerning capital mobility. Yet we have seen that capital and labour mobility are not simple alternatives, just as trade and factor mobility are not simple alternatives. The whole question of diversity of regulations needs to be considered more fully and this will be done in the next section.

5.3 Trade and diversity

In the context of the trading block, a leading issue is how to respond, if indeed a response is required, to diversity within the union. The market model says that diversity is fine, the more the better, for diversity is the source of comparative advantage, price deviations and strong gains from trade. More strictly, the answer has to depend on what is diverse. Diverse tastes, diverse costs, etc., are the things that produce gains from trade. Comparative advantage may be defined in terms of differences in relative prices prior to trade. Where such price differentials exist in an economy without government interventions and taxes, trade will be gainful. Yet the same may not be true when initial price differences are partly accounted for by taxes, tariffs and differential regulation. We saw something like that with the simple Viner example of Chapter 3, properly interpreted. Before the customs union between Arcadia and Bella is formed, these two countries have different relative prices for food and wine, so that it appears that more trade between them would be gainful. Yet such is not the case, as we have seen, at least not for more trade between Arcadia and Bella. The distortions caused by all the tariffs account for this fact. Price differentials affected by tariffs do not measure true social costs.[8]

Diverse regulations, tariffs and rules, however, can easily produce misallocation and inefficiency. Suppose, for example, that some countries are relaxed and easy about any harm that production may do to the environment. Then those countries will attract 'dirty' industries. Possibly the said countries have a genuinely different value system that attaches a low cost to damage to the environment. Yet the same relaxed attitude to the environment might be a trade-diverting policy to attract industries that, for all their dirtiness, may have, or be seen to have, valued external economies, such as employment generation or the saving of adjustment costs.

Government subsidy also raises issues of regulation harmony. The problem arises because of increasing returns, a point that will be developed in Chapter 6. Over the last twenty years there has been a significant shift in economists' attitudes to the mechanisms of protection, a shift that reflects intellectual fashion to some extent, but also changes in institutions during the same period. The old textbook argument used to say that tariff protection is a highly inferior means even of keeping an industry going when the existence of that industry is desired as a non-economic objective. A subsidy is better than a tariff, said the theory of commercial policy.

Subsidies, however, can be and have been causes of international trade friction. In the traditional commercial policy models, production subsidies did no harm to trading partners, at least no long-term harm. If industry I is subsidized, this will provide good I to the trading partner at lower cost and the burdens will fall on the country paying the subsidy. True there may be losses to particular factors – Stolper–Samuelson or specific factor costs. These have been of great importance. Otherwise one might ask why the USA is so concerned about the harm done to its farmers by the CAP policy of the EC. True the harm to the farmers is evident, but they are few as a proportion of the population and could be compensated. More importantly, it might be thought, the CAP anti-protects European manufacturing and service activity, which the USA, given its current concerns, might be expected to welcome.

This last example concerns two large countries or blocks. Much of traditional commercial policy theory is addressed to the small-country case in which what the policy is has a large effect on the home country and little effect on the world outside. That is often unrealistic and will certainly be so among the countries that form a block. Then rent and profit capture could easily be serious problems as the member countries of the union vie with each other to attract a desirable industry. These issues can be considered fully only in models of large industries and increasing returns. Such models are the subject of the next chapter.

If one government allows its firms to pollute the environment and others strictly forbid it, block-wide misallocation of resources may result. That would certainly be the case if the light application of environmental regulation were to be used as an instrument of protection. The issues are more difficult if countries have different tastes regarding environmental goods and bads. These may be determined by local environmental conditions. For example, acid rain is particularly harmful in Scandinavian conditions, because soils are thin and acid, so that natural buffering is poor, while forest cover is high. Or the differences in tastes may be accounted for by income differences. Rich countries typically care more about environmental goods than do poor countries. Or cultural influences may play a role.

In such cases it seems as though trade can be gainful if production activities go to where their external diseconomies impose the least costs.[9] The outcome will not be good, however, if environmental regulation is combined with a tendency to protection for the kind of political economic reason discussed above. Suppose, as an illustrative example, that the steel manufacture is a declining industry with high adjustment costs (say in the form of the unemployment of laid-off workers) plus negative environmental diseconomies. In such a case the Nash equilibrium of non-cooperative environmental regulation by several countries will be inefficient. By allowing a little more pollution than is optimal given own output and every other country's output, any country gains because it maintains steel output at a higher level and exports excess capacity and labour unemployment. As this is true for all, the final equilibrium has too much pollution for all countries relative to the ideal coordinated equilibrium of environmental regulation. The example is reinforced if slack regulation attracts inward investment.

It is very important to understand, particularly in the context of a trade block, the distinction between coordination of regulations for the sake of efficiency and the implementation of like regulations for the sake of uniformity. The imposition of uniformity will be inefficient if countries differ. Equally, lack of coordination of regulation will be inefficient because the equilibrium of a non-cooperative game is usually inefficient. That is fine as a textbook distinction but applying these principles in practice may run into difficulties. A group of rational countries in a block agree to differ according to varying environmental tastes but to coordinate optimally. Now, because the cooperative equilibrium is not a Nash equilibrium, it pays an unscrupulous country to pretend to care less about the environment than it really does in order to end up with a larger steel industry with its partners paying part of the cost.

Clearly every case is different. An evident danger, with which the EC flirted in the negotiations to define the Maastricht Treaty, is that rich high-productivity countries will attempt to protect some of their industries by exporting via regulation their own high net advantage wages to countries with low productivity. This is not mainly a defence of the British opt-out from the Social Chapter of the Maastricht Treaty, although that may be defensible. More to the present point, the proposal was considerably diluted in the course of the negotiations. For instance, a Community-wide minimum wage originally proposed was dropped. Some poorer countries may have become anxious about such schemes, but the main effect will have been worries on the part of rich and powerful countries that regulations imposing uniform standards simply would not work, if only because poorer countries are unlikely to apply regulations strongly to their disadvantage.

It is to be hoped that inside the EC the tensions caused by diversity do not translate to more straightforward protection, including interference with the operation of the single market. Yet the route of protection to defend high wage levels is already being practised by the EC in its relations with newly liberated Eastern Europe. As a long-term strategy that cannot work. The opening up of Eastern Europe is equivalent to a huge supply shock, for Europe particularly, the supply concerned being of well-educated labour with low opportunity cost. The idea that West European real wages might long be insulated from this shock is unconvincing. Stolper–Samuelson-style protection will not do the job because in the modern world mobile capital will flow away from a high-wage region, reducing the wage level originally boosted by protection to the rate sustainable in the long run for the country concerned.

A similar case to the environmental regulation example discussed above is encountered if different countries regulate employment conditions more or less strictly with respect to such matters as safety, health effects and employment security. If one takes the view that the regulations make good imperfections in private markets, then haphazard compliance will distort the allocation of resources in a haphazard way, as with the environment. If different employment regulations reflect the social tastes of different governments and peoples, then they point to a basis for gainful exchange. Except for technical issues, there is no fundamental difference between the regulation of wage levels and the regulation of employment conditions. The majority of EC governments have argued themselves into an inconsistent position according to which employment conditions should be regulated in the direction of uniformity but not wage rates.

Wage-rate convergence and migration within a trading block are obviously interrelated, because, if wages are uniform and jobs are available at those wages, the incentive to migrate is reduced. Mass migration may not appeal to governments. It has happened and been welcomed in the USA, but it occurs much less readily in Europe or Japan. Again, emigration from low-productivity regions may ameliorate unemployment in those regions. If an individual decides to migrate, this will often be a simple improvement in the allocation of resources, now including people. If a young Manchester resident boards an aeroplane to Frankfurt looking for a better life, he is revealing a preference for life in Frankfurt over life in Manchester. He hopes to find a Frankfurt employer who will pay him a higher wage than he can earn in Manchester. And that employer, if he exists, is valuing the labour more highly than the Manchester alternative.

It is seldom that simple. There are serious uncertainties and externalities, and migration will be something about which value judgements differ. The survival of local cultures and life-styles is at issue. But more direct economic costs also arise. Migration-receiving regions may become congested, with serious external economies such as road traffic congestion. Depopulated regions may suffer from local tax revenue loss and a consequent decline in public services and infrastructure. Migration is not something about which governments can be unconcerned, and it is not something about which they should be unconcerned.

5.4 Regional policy

A single market trading block is in many ways like a large nation. Large nations typically have regional problems; difficulties that arise because the experience of economic development in various parts of the country proves to be uneven. Some of these problems tend to sort themselves out if enough time is allowed for market processes to have their effect. Regions adapt to their comparative advantages. Migration may move people to places where their economic prospects are better. Above all, the general economic situation changes and this can alter the relative position of different regions surprisingly and dramatically. In nineteenth-century Britain, the southern counties experienced marked industrial decline as their traditional craft production proved incapable of competing with the factory manufacturing of the North. After the First World War their relative position improved when they became the sites of electric and motor manufacturing. In the USA, the South has enjoyed a relative economic revival since the Second World War. Other regions have seen depopulation ameliorate some of their pressing regional problem status. The Highlands of Scotland might provide such an example.

Leaving time and natural processes of adjustment to take care of regional problems is a slow and uncertain way of solving them. Very often governments prefer to intervene to try to improve upon the *laissez-faire* outcome. Typical interventions include investment subsidies, tax concessions, favoured status for government expenditure and more besides. The EC has developed more than one programme to transfer funds to less favoured regions. These include the structural funds and the cohesion funds. The idea is that centralised expenditures should enable relatively less favoured regions to come closer to the general level of development in the Community. This aim is already present in the law and practice of the EC.

Similar schemes have long operated in individual countries in Europe and elsewhere. They are important to Italy in particular, a country of sharply divergent regional situations, and conceivably precarious unity. A feature that Italian regional policy and the regional policy of the EC share is that expenditure is targeted on infrastructure expenditure. Italian regional policy has also included the location of public production in backward areas. Neither Italy nor the EC makes direct subsidy of private sector activity part of the regional policy. Other nations, including the UK, have also had regional policies. Notice that such expenditures are the nearest we come in practice to the idealised lump-sum compensation that allows the textbook model to make a trading block generally beneficial. They are a very poor approximation to the ideal and it must be noted that, generally speaking, publicly organised regional policies have been notably unsuccessful. There is, in particular, no evidence that the centralised dispersion of limited funding can create a situation in which backward regions can compete with wage levels comparable to those of richer regions.

Regional policy of a large trading block, such as the EC, is not different in kind from the regional policy of a nation, such as Italy or Britain. Therefore it is important and relevant to note that national regional policies have generally been unsuccessful. Reasons why the experience of regional policies has been disappointing include the following:

- policies have been under-funded and poorly focused; they are under-funded because regional policies that really affect location of industries and large numbers of jobs are very expensive;
- they have been ill focused because politicians do not select narrow and clear objectives (e.g. employment creation) and direct policy to achieve those particular objectives;

- equalising wages and employment conditions discourages the migration of labour only if jobs are obtainable in poorer regions with the improved conditions; otherwise it encourages migration.

5.5 Capital mobility

Capital mobility is an important substitute for labour mobility. When goods and capital can move freely within the trade block, the need for labour to migrate is reduced. Spanish workers producing Volkswagen cars in Seville have no motive to migrate to Germany. In Europe, particularly, labour migration has not been a great force for economic adaptation and convergence. Unlike in the USA, cultural and linguistic barriers to mobility, while they are far from complete blocks to labour mobility, do constitute substantial barriers. Why worry? With capital mobility being high in the world at large, and in Europe too, why can we not depend on capital to go to labour and to equalise factor incomes, or at least to reduce inequalities substantially? Capital mobility in the EC is more or less uninhibited by legal restrictions by virtue of Articles 67 and 68 of the Rome Treaty and associated regulations.[10] With the legal framework liberal, what more is needed? That we cannot depend on capital to do this is evident from observation. What is the theoretical reason for this fact?

The Heckscher–Ohlin model, or rather its antithesis, provides the answer. If the assumptions of that model – constant returns to scale, the same technology in every country, perfect information and no transport costs – did describe reality, then capital mobility would not be needed, because trade would equalise factor prices without capital moving, but capital mobility would also do the job perfectly and give complete regional convergence. In fact none of the critical assumptions is satisfied, not even approximately. In particular, increasing returns to scale and agglomeration economies exert powerful influences on the location of industry. To produce far from the market, and in economically marginal regions, is certainly not impossible, as Volkswagen has demonstrated in Andalucia, and Nissan has shown in North-East England. Yet it is never simple. Also, another Heckscher–Ohlin assumption, homogeneity of labour, is seriously violated in many cases. Not only do the skills, experience and training of workers vary widely across regions, but these patterns tend, naturally, to reinforce rather than to moderate pre-existing patterns of regional specialisation. There is no point in a young worker in deep rural France obtaining training for industrial employment unless he or she plans to migrate. And if the social inhibitions to migration are strong, there is no point in acquiring training useful only for industrial or high-tech service employment.

Arguments of this type might seem to point to the conclusion that the superficial identification of the free movement of capital with economic efficiency is questionable. By way of illustration, consider the owner of a factory in Portugal deciding whether to sell up and invest the proceeds in a company that will produce in France. Despite the fact that the sale price of the factory will be low, because it will cease production and its premises will be used for storage, the relocation of his capital looks attractive to the factory owner. Two types of external effects may be important here, and they pull in opposite directions. First, the capital movement takes capital to where its private marginal productivity is higher. This is internalised in the investor's decision. Next there are external economies in the French region receiving the capital (possibly external congestion diseconomies too). Finally, there will typically be external diseconomies in the Portuguese region that is losing capital. As some of these important effects are neither taken into account by the private investor nor, realistically, offset by optimal public interventions, free capital mobility looks non-optimal in principle.

On grounds of pure theory, that would be the correct conclusion. It is easy to construct an example with increasing returns and external economies in which location of capital by optimal planned allocation would improve on the market outcome. Yet the practical case is likely to come down in favour of free mobility, even if ideal controls on capital mobility might theoretically make things better. The crucial point is that apparently realistic examples, showing how controls could improve outcomes, tend to make unrealistic assumptions about information available to the administrator, and about that same administrator's independence from pressures from parties interested in influencing the outcome.

Our conclusions seem to be discouraging. What free capital mobility can achieve is limited. It is an imperfect substitute for perfect labour mobility. And in itself it does not invariably improve the allocation of resources. On the other hand, the main problems with free capital mobility are external economies and diseconomies, including those associated with labour market inflexibilities, increasing returns and congestion costs. Ideally, none of these problems would be addressed by capital controls, but by more direct interventions.

5.6 A migration analogue of the Kemp–Wan result

Consider the now familiar case of three countries: our old friends Arcadia, Bella and Extra. Now we take the tariffs on trade between these countries as fixed and allow trade flows to take place as their residents choose. Initially the three countries have given supplies of factors. Think in particular of labour, which will always be a potentially mobile factor in this argument. We also start from a presumption that migration is beneficial. We have already seen that this does not have to be the case. One can certainly invent examples in which the external diseconomies caused by migration are quantitatively more important than the benefits that the migrants register when they decide to migrate. Such examples just produce cases equivalent to the degenerate instances of the Kemp–Wan theorem in which there are no gains from trade between the countries that form the customs union. External diseconomies make such cases more common, but there is no difference in principle.

Migration is regulated in this model by a vector of 'migration charges', which function like tariffs. One does not have to think of charges as literally monetary charges. They represent the whole gamut of restrictions and regulations governing migration: quotas, qualification rules, mutual recognition of professional accreditation, whatever. But let honesty declare that for this argument to work a continuity assumption is required that may not be realistic for migration regulation. For migration regulation is riddled with discontinuities.

Ignoring this point, consider the situation when Arcadia and Bella form a free-migration union. This means that labour and other factors can migrate freely within the union, and this is assumed to confer benefits in terms of increased efficiency in the location of labour. By analogy to the Kemp–Wan theorem, one needs to assume that the losers from free migration will be compensated by means of lump-sum transfers. If free emigration is a Pareto improvement then, by definition, all may gain if transfers are taken into account. These gains are assumed to be available while migration from the outside world (Extra) is held constant.

The idea of this, admittedly informal, argument is that migration quantities from the outside world will have shadow prices just as goods trades have shadow prices in the Kemp–Wan argument. Those shadow prices will define changes in the common vector of migration charges that will hold immigration of factors constant. The sketch of a result is less than a theorem. For we cannot draw on a precise mathematical framework that makes factor migration exactly similar to trade in goods and services – not without making unrealistic assumptions – particularly not without making convexity assumptions, which are simply out of place for the factor migration case.

While the theorem is doubtful, not all the conclusions to which it points are wrong. It is correct to conclude, for instance, that there are migration analogues for trade creation and trade diversion. If a trade block allows free migration of factors this makes gains possible. On the other hand, migration may be diverted from outside the block to inside the block, and this may not represent an increase in efficiency. If, for instance, the European single market allows Portuguese workers to migrate to Germany, these migrant workers may replace workers from Turkey. A chauvinistic philosophy might seem to point to the conclusion that this could be hard luck for the Turkish workers but could not involve harm to the selfish interest of the block residents.

When implications for trade of factor migration are taken into account, this last conclusion need not be valid. Factor migration affects trade, contracting industries using emigrant factors intensively. So a switch from Turkish to Portuguese migrants might contract the supply of port wine to Europe and increase relatively the supply of dried apricots – to take a frivolous illustration, but one with the right structure. If that switch is a bad change, then the factor migration diversion may be inefficient even from the selfish point of view of block insiders.

5.7 Conclusions

The most helpful approach views factor migration as closely analogous to the exchange of goods and services in trade. In the most abstract model, the Arrow–Debreu general equilibrium model, that is the only way that migration can be represented, although there are problems, as was noted. In that context it is important to note that perfect competitive markets do not imply easy mobility of labour services, any more than perfect competitive markets for trousers and skirts will imply that these goods will be close substitutes. Capital might be thought to be more perfectly mobile in principle because it seeks a high return, not maximum utility, and high return is more indifferent to location. Against that go differences in information, which are not independent of location, and local scale economies, which encourage concentration of investment in certain points in space.

Factor mobility tends to be associated with external economies (of scale, and rent creation and conglomeration) and diseconomies (of local congestion and regional decline in areas denied investment). Hence non-intervention can easily be shown to be non-optimal on theoretical grounds. That intervention, however, should not be addressed to factor mobility as such, for that is not where the problems originate. And, in any case, the fine-tuning of capital movements, like the fine-tuning of regulations, is open to abuse, for affected governments too easily use such degrees of freedom as instruments for disguised protection.

Notes

1 Malinvaud (1985, pp. 22–3) notes that location in space creates non-convexities in preferences or in production feasibility. His example involves the comparison of either the same lunch eaten in Paris or Lyons, or half the lunch eaten in Paris and half of it eaten in Lyons.
2 They are essential to Paul Krugman's economic geography. See Krugman (1991b).
3 See Tiebout (1956), Rubinfield (1987) and Stiglitz (1983).
4 The Articles are 48–73. See Rudden and Wyatt (1993), pp. 48–54 and 290–309.
5 The transfers concerned go under the name of the structural funds, cohesion funds or other titles according to the precise purposes and rules for distribution.
6 See Rybczynski (1955).
7 The literature, primary and secondary, is vast. For an introduction, see Caves, Frankel and Jones (1993), Chapter 7; Dixit and Norman (1980), pp. 110–26; and Ethier (1988), Chapter 3.
8 One could qualify that statement by saying that even policy-distorted price differentials may allow for gainful exchange if suitable instruments can be found. Such is not the case in the simple Viner example, became the case with its extension embodying substitution in consumption, and could apply again with a Kemp–Wan union.
9 As is argued by Bhagwati and Srinivasan (1993).
10 See Rudden and Wyatt (1993), p. 54.

CHAPTER 6

Imperfect competition, increasing returns and strategic trade

6.1 Imperfect competition and increasing returns

This chapter looks at some of the implications of large producers and increasing returns to scale for the theory of trading blocks and for related policy issues. As is well known, trade theory has been transformed during the course of the last decade by the introduction of models, often borrowed initially from industrial economics, that include these features. This is now a large field and the following discussion, rather than providing a comprehensive treatment, has the aim of giving the flavour of the type of result available in the context of trade block formation.[1]

Central to the new theory are imperfect competition and increasing returns to scale, and the two assumptions go together. Increasing returns will often mean that a market can support only a small number of producers, who will not be even approximately perfectly competitive. Equally, to make the number of producers a significant variable in a model we typically need to attach a cost to the proliferation of producers. Otherwise the number can be assumed to be as large as is needed to provide competition – a free entry assumption ensures that – or as large as is required to provide whatever variety of goods for which there is a demand, because without non-convexities there is no cost to an indefinite proliferation of variety.

Imperfect competition can refer to more than one thing in economics: either any market in which the individual producer is not an atomistic price-taker, or the familiar type of Chamberlain model in which a producer is small in the economy but large in a local market. I shall concentrate my attention on a small number of large producers (monopolists or oligopolists) because I can do everything that I need to do in that framework. Models with large producers will be called oligopoly models, as a general term is useful. So monopoly is a special case of oligopoly, either monopoly in the world as a whole or monopoly in one national market. Oligopolists like to spread their sales out across markets, so oligopoly leads to cross-hauling, which in this context means trade for the sake of adding sales in a different market.

There is little literature on how the classic customs union question is affected by imperfect competition and increasing returns. However Corden (1972) analyses the effect of customs union formation with increasing returns. By contemporary standards his analytical methods are rudimentary; yet he arrived at the essential insight that large markets attract production, owing to the scale effect, and that this can both promote and divert trade.[2]

6.2 A customs union model

Consider a very simple model of a customs union. In each of three countries, called again Arcadia, Bella and Extra (shortened to A, B and E), there is one product, 'food', produced by labour under constant returns to scale and by numerous competitive producers, and identical 'cars', produced by one oligopolistic firm in each country. At the start all countries impose a tariff on the import of cars at rate t. The tariff is levied in terms of food. Hence t is the amount of food that has to be paid to the government of the importing country per car imported. The home government uses this food for its own purposes, or gives it out to home residents. There are no transport costs.

An equilibrium condition for cross-hauling holds regardless of how much output any car producer generates. The net marginal revenue must be the same in each market. Assume that a producer who wants to sell in a market delivers his output to that market, when the price on the market is determined by an inverse demand curve. In deciding how much output to sell in any market, a producer treats the sales of other producers on that market as given. In standard terminology, a Nash–Cournot equilibrium is assumed. Producers are treated as if they have infinite capacities and choose outputs unconstrained. With a single market, an equally valid, and possibly better, interpretation of the Cournot quantity-setting oligopoly model is to suppose that producers choose capacities in the knowledge that price competition will drive them to sell up to capacity in that market. A similar interpretation is available when the seller provides sales for many markets. The producer chooses a capacity sufficient to provide for all the markets in the knowledge that price competition will drive production up to the

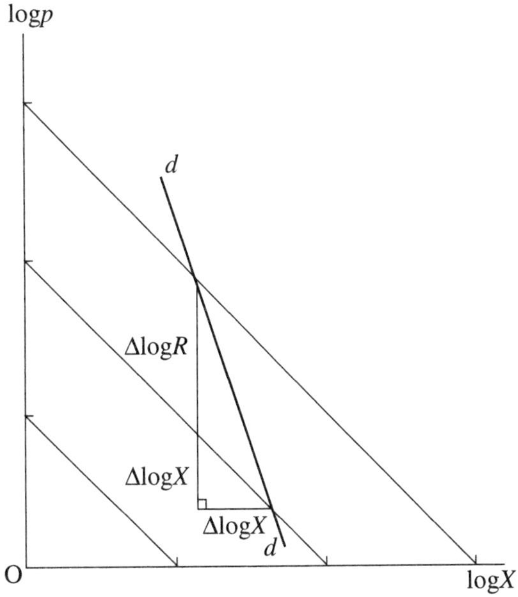

Figure 6.1

total capacity when the marginal profitability of unit sales is equated across markets.

In the market of any country, a producer, not necessarily resident in that country, is selling cars. What is the producer's marginal revenue? The answer is shown on a figure here, leaving a mathematical demonstration to the appendix to this chapter. Let our producer increase his sales to the market by a small amount. What is the resulting change in revenue? The answer is shown on Figure 6.1, which shows what is happening in terms of the relationship between the logarithms of total sales to the market log X and the logarithm of price log p. Once the market marginal revenue is established, it is easy to show how the marginal revenue of one seller, who accounts for only part of total sales, may be determined.

The figure shows the market demand curve for cars in the form of the relationship between log X and log p as the heavy curve *dd*. This is drawn as a straight line for convenience, but more than convenience is involved to tell the truth. For the argument only works, and only succeeds in by-passing the need for the calculus, if the demand curve in logs is approximately linear, at least locally, which is the same as saying that the elasticity of demand, which is the negative of the inverse slope of the demand curve in logs, does not vary too much. The lighter downward-sloping lines on the figure have slope -1. Hence they show loci of points along which $\log X + \log p$ is constant, and that is the same as saying that $p.X$, revenue, is constant. The logarithm of revenue is measured by the vertical intercept. On the figure, the triangle shown measures the effect of a change in sales shown as $\Delta \log X$ being the base of the triangle. As the negative slope of *dd* is the elasticity of demand ϵ, we have:

$$\frac{1}{\epsilon} = \frac{\Delta \log X + \Delta \log R}{\Delta \log X} \tag{6.1}$$

where R is revenue. Hence:

$$\Delta \log R = \Delta \log X . \left[1 - \frac{1}{\epsilon}\right] \tag{6.2}$$

As $\Delta \log X = \Delta X/X$ and $\Delta \log R = \Delta R/R$, the expression (6.2) can be arranged to give:

$$\Delta R = p.X. \frac{\Delta X}{X} . \left[1 - \frac{1}{\epsilon}\right] = \Delta X.p. \left[1 - \frac{1}{\epsilon}\right] \tag{6.3}$$

This formula gives marginal revenue for an expansion of sales to the whole market. To translate this to marginal revenue for a single seller given the sales levels of other producers is easy enough. The inverse of the elasticity of demand measures the proportionate reduction in the price consequent on a given proportionate increase in supply to the market. Then, obviously, the elasticity for an individual seller is lower, because a given percentage increase in his sales represents a smaller percentage increase in total sales and, obviously, the inverse elasticity is reduced in proportion to the individual seller's share of total market sales. If a seller's market share is 25%, the inverse elasticity for that seller acting alone will be one quarter of the market inverse elasticity. Hence marginal revenue for an individual seller is:

$$\Delta R = \Delta X.p. \left[1 - \frac{s}{\epsilon}\right] \tag{6.4}$$

where $s = x/X$ where x is the individual seller's sales and X is total sales.

Notice that the relation given, by equating the rate of change of market price with respect to the sales of a single producer to a market-share-weighted rate of change for the whole market, implicitly assumes that the individual producer computes gross marginal revenue treating the sales of other producers as constants. To state the assumption explicitly, we are looking for a Nash equilibrium in the quantities sold by the various producers on this market.

With the principles according to which gross marginal revenue is computed clarified, note that producers will sell quantities such that gross marginal revenue is equal to marginal cost, denoted *m*. Hence we have:

$$\Delta X.m = \Delta R = \Delta X.p.\left[1 - \frac{s}{\epsilon}\right] \tag{6.5}$$

The equation shows, however, that the only way for gross marginal revenues to vary between producers is for their market shares to vary. These variations, in turn, can be related only to differences in marginal costs. Marginal costs may vary for all or any of numerous reasons. Costs of production may differ because of differences in efficiency, or on account of different scales of operation. Costs of delivering cars to a particular market will be affected by transport costs and by tariffs.

In any case, rearranging (6.5), the implications of cost differences for market shares are made clear. The equation implies:

$$s = \epsilon\left(\frac{p - m}{p}\right) \tag{6.6}$$

From which we may derive immediately:

Theorem 6.1: *With all sellers in a market in a Nash equilibrium of sales levels, market shares are inversely related to marginal costs of producing and delivering to that market.*

The theorem applies generally, whenever more than one firm sells in the same market. The same method may be applied to a case that has the same structure as the Viner customs union model. There are three countries, in each of which there is one large producer, and each of which at the start levies a tariff on the import of cars at rate *t* (in terms of food). Now two of the countries form a customs union, so that cars may be exported from one to the other without paying any tariff. This reduces the marginal cost of selling into the other union country for each firm in the union. Lower marginal costs mean higher market shares. Therefore firms inside the union interpenetrate each other's markets to a greater extent. Indeed if there are no transport costs, or other asymmetries, they will sell as much in the other union country market as they sell at home. The third country will lose market share in both countries of the union. With quantity-setting Nash equilibrium, customs union formation is import substituting.

These results are summarized in the next theorem.

Theorem 6.2: *Each oligopolist will have a larger share (hence larger than a third share in the symmetrical case) of the home market than of the foreign market, and the deviation from equality will be larger the smaller is marginal cost divided by price for home producers relative to the same ratio for outside producers.*

The theorem assumes a pure strategy Nash equilibrium in sales levels in each market to have been established. Yet our equilibrium condition applies to a single producer and gives that producer's share of total sales. Obviously, for each market, the shares of total sales for all producers should sum to 1. That need not imply that the system is over-determined, as an example computed in the appendix below demonstrates. Even so, it will be clear that the existence of a Nash equilibrium with several quantity-setting sellers is not something that can be established with a wave of the hand. To get a sense of the nature of the possible mathematical problems it is helpful to think, not in terms of market shares, but in terms of the underlying game that the producers play in output quantities. The basic problems have to do with boundedness of the space of relevant production/sales levels, on the one hand, and discontinuities of production-level responses to other producers' production levels, on the other. Without one or other of these problems intervening, a fixed-point argument will show the existence of at least one Nash equilibrium.

Non-existence of Nash equilibrium due to unboundedness occurs in the case of two producers with zero production costs, no tariffs and a unit elasticity of demand in each market, so that total sales revenue in each market is a constant. As each producer takes a larger share of the revenue going if he increases his sales there relative to the sales of his competitor, and as he does so at no cost, there can be no equilibrium in which both producers do not wish to increase their sales in each market. If there is an upper limit on a producer's sales, both sell this amount and the oligopolistic solution is the same as the competitive solution. The problem of unboundedness seems to be more a technical issue than a serious practical difficulty for this type of analysis.

The possibility of discontinuities in sales reaction functions has to be taken more seriously, as it could undermine the existence of a pure strategy equilibrium in a way that could not be fixed up, as could be done in the unboundedness example. Such discontinuities have been demonstrated in the literature for regular cases.[3] As it is not easy to interpret mixed-strategy solutions as descriptions of actual divisions of sales between different national producers, we shall assume that a pure strategy Nash equilibrium in sales levels exists.

The model confirms the well-known result that oligopoly in international trade generates cross-hauling. Cross-hauling means that producers often sell into each other's national markets, simply because, were they not to do so, gross marginal revenues would vary between different markets with similar prices more than the differences in the cost of delivering to those markets. This may be seen by setting $s = 0$ in (6.5), when it is clear that gross marginal revenue in a market in which a producer sells nothing is the market price. And, for oligopolists, market price exceeds marginal cost. The model tells us that tariffs, by decreasing marginal revenue to foreign sellers, protect home oligopolists. Consumers, however, suffer from this protection because less cross-hauling means higher car prices in the home market. Cross-hauling in a symmetrical model with transport costs (absent from my example) is wasteful and this might seem to point to the conclusion that it is a bad thing and that a tariff that limited the extent to which it takes place would be a good idea. In fact the issue is more complicated than such a simple account would suggest. Consumers' benefits from increased competition have to be offset against the wastes of useless trade and the loss of producers' surplus due to lower car prices.

6.3 Profitability, exit and industrial policy

The presentation of producer equilibrium in a model of international trading oligopolists has been extremely parsimonious, working just from equal net marginal revenue conditions for sales into different markets. That involved some analytical cheating, as was explained, because the argument assumed the existence of a pure strategy Nash equilibrium in sales levels, without demonstrating existence. Even so, the argument derived valid necessary conditions for a pure strategy Nash quantity-setting equilibrium in which all producers sell in all markets. The conditions can easily be extended to allow for zero sales into a market in which the price is equal to, or lower than, the total marginal cost of selling into that market.

Even extended, however, the equilibrium conditions are far from being sufficient conditions for long-run general equilibrium. We also need to look at the overall equilibrium situation of the producer. To examine the most simple possible case, assume that each producer has the same cost function:

$$C = \alpha + \beta y \tag{6.7}$$

where C is total costs of production, y is output, and α and β are positive constants. Think of α as large, which will explain the oligopolistic structure of the industry. The level of constant marginal production cost, β, affects market share by influencing marginal production cost m, and, for given sales and prices, high marginal costs reduce the gross profit available before overhead costs have been paid for. Whether a producer will continue to operate in the industry depends on whether it can make enough gross profit to pay its overhead costs.

Let us return to the three-country model in a perfect symmetrical equilibrium constructed for convenience of exposition and analysis. Arcadia, Bella and Extra each have one producer and each charge the same tariff on car imports. Now A and B form a customs union and the tariff rate on car imports from A into B, or from B into A, goes to zero. What does the union do to the profitability of car production for producers inside the customs union?

The effect of the customs union for the profitability of the car producers inside it are complex. Suppose for the moment, however, that all three car producers survive and consider the equilibrium that will result. We can see from the equilibrium condition that A and B's car producers will gain market share in each other's markets and then it is easily seen that E will lose share in both those markets. The greater competition inside the union will cause car prices to fall; this is what discourages E's producer from selling in the union market. The greater competition and lower price inside the union are bad for the total profit generated by all car sales in the union. Yet now producers in the union will take a larger share of what profit is going. That suggests, as is indeed the case, that the profits of inside-union car producers may rise or may fall. A complete demonstration of this point is provided in the appendix.

That a decline in profitability is possible is easily demonstrated. Suppose that A, B and E are symmetrical and initially the tariff level is higher than the difference between the monopoly price for any country and marginal production cost. Then each producer is a monopolist in the home market, exports nothing, and total profit is monopoly profit in one of the markets, call it P. Now A and B form a customs union, interpenetrate each other's markets and car prices fall. Certainly that will not lead to E exporting to A or B, while the home market of E, which still has the original tariff, remains protected. With competition in each of the markets of A and B, total profit is less than P. By symmetry the A and B producers take equal shares of these markets, ending up with total profits of twice one half of something less than P, which can only be less than P in total.

Noting that it is only one possibility, suppose that the profits of A's and B's car producers fall, because, as in the example above, their gain from lower competition from E's producer is more than offset by their stronger competition with each other. The fall in profits is the other side of the gain to A's and B's consumers, who now enjoy lower car prices. Whether producers in A and B can take a cut in profits depends on the value of α, the cost of overheads. If gross profits before the customs union was formed were only just above α, then the increased competition within the union will drive one producer out of business. If we assume, unlike the example above, that E is crowded out of A's and B's markets, the logical assumption is that E's producer will go out of business, since its situation is definitely the worst of what were previously a symmetrical and identical three. In that case a customs union will cut out imports of extra-union cars and will indeed promote exports of cars out of the union into E. A customs union is export promoting.

This looks like trade diversion but it is not classic trade diversion. Standard trade diversion consists in a customs union pulling production and trade flows away from comparative advantage, with consequent costs to domestic or foreign welfare. That is not what is happening here. As a completely symmetrical situation prior to the formation of the customs union was chosen, there is no comparative advantage as such. The presence of increasing returns to scale (overheads are less burdensome when spread across more output) means that producer elimination is a move towards world efficiency, so, if we followed Viner's original method, concentrating on the issue of whether a customs union promotes world efficiency, we would count the outcome in which E's producer is eliminated as a good thing. It makes more sense to look at the effect of the customs union on the welfare of consumers in the various countries. Then the answer is ambiguous.

Consumers in A and B gain. They get their cars cheaper because the two producers in A and B cross-haul without a tariff restricting that. Consumers in E are worse off, because they lose a tariff-free national producer and our assumption is that E keeps on the tariff against car inputs, although that has lost whatever reason it ever had.

Now suppose that the producer in E cannot be driven out of business. Perhaps its government subsidises its production to make up for the lost profit, a loss accounted for by the fact that it is now exporting into more competitive, more difficult foreign markets. Then it is natural to suppose that one of the producers in A or B will go out of business. Which one? The model cannot say, for it has created an indeterminacy by setting up a simple symmetry, while at the same time not including in the model dynamic or other factors that might explain which car industry will fail. No matter: one will fail; let it be the producer in Bella.

Now only Arcadia in the customs union has a car industry. What has happened is that the Arcadia car industry has become a monopolist of the larger joint market Arcadia plus Bella. It is not a strict monopolist because it still has to compete with imports from Extra; but Extra competes at a disadvantage because of the common external tariff on car imports, still assumed to be levied. Free from the irksome cross-hauling competition from B, the car producer of A will sell less than the previous combined sales of the car producer of A plus the car producer of B, raising car prices in the union. This reduction in sales in turn will lead to the car producer of E selling more cars in the union. The slack competition pulls in imports.

An industry asking for protection often argues in terms something like this: The government, consumers' organisation, whoever, may think that buyers will benefit when cheap imports are allowed in. Once those imports have come in, and local producers have been driven out of business, however, prices will go right back up again and higher still. Such arguments are sometimes plainly self-serving, and they are often couched in terms that suggest that a commercial conspiracy is involved in which the initial low pricing is deliberately intended to force local producers out of business – the so-called predatory behaviour.

What happens in the model just presented is not this precisely. There is no predation: firms are assumed to maximise current profits as Cournot–Nash players. Yet what an observer in Bella experiences is a history quite similar to the predatory story. First A and B merge their economies into a customs union. Car producers in both countries predict dire consequences, especially the Bella producer, which perhaps knows that its own financial resources are such that it will lose in a competitive battle to stay in car production. The two car producers of the customs union compete with each other more effectively in the other union market and car prices come down. But the financial press reports that Bella-cars, the car producer of Bella, is in serious financial difficulties, and in due course it closes down.

Now Arcadia-cars has a partial monopoly of the union market; partial because Extra-cars competes with it across the tariff barrier. Before the union, Arcadia-cars was competing with two foreign producers who had to cross its tariff barrier. It now sells to a market twice as large. As overhead costs affect only whether a producer stays in production or not, but do not affect profit-maximising outputs, the effect of the customs union is the same as if Arcadia-cars and Bella-cars had formed a cartel to maximise their joint profits in Arcadia and Bella. Not surprisingly, the cartel would sell fewer cars than would the two producers with uncoordinated cross competition. So car prices in the customs union end up higher than they would be without the union.

Although the example is a highly stylised simple example, it is interesting to ask what policy lessons follow from it. If the governments of the trading block foresee the unfortunate outcome described, there are various policy interventions that they might employ.

- they could establish an industrial policy that would subsidise the weaker car producer to keep it in business for the sake of competition;
- if the two producers can survive inside the union but they plan to merge to coordinate their joint production, competition policy can prohibit this;
- if the union will end up with one car producer, the union's external tariff can be lowered to allow Extra-cars to compete more effectively with Arcadia-cars.

Which policy intervention is best if only the selfish interests of the block countries are taken into account? That question will be complicated in practice by adjustment costs. If a car producer closes down, the workers will not melt costlessly into food production. To keep things simple, however, ignore that difficulty. Another simplifying assumption is to suppose that all the residents of each nation are identical to all other residents of the same nation. Hence car production profit is distributed to everyone. Then a national welfare function has just two arguments, national income measured in terms of food and the food price of cars. National income is:

$$F + P - \alpha \tag{6.8}$$

where F is the maximum food production of the nation, P is gross operating profits of the national car producer (if there is one), and the α for overhead costs is deducted only if there is a national car producer. The reason why F, maximum food production, appears in the equation even if some workers are employed making cars is that the constant marginal productivity of workers in producing food sets the food wage rate, so that F is national wage income in fact.

For these reasons, when we make partial comparisons of national welfare, we reach the following conclusion. National welfare is higher the larger are net profits from car production and the lower is the price of cars. The complication for policy design is that the two vital variables cannot usually be selected independently. They tend to pull against each other.

Consider our menu of policy choices again. An industrial policy keeps a weak car producer in business. We can think of it as a means of allowing net profits from car production to be negative, which would normally be inconsistent with equilibrium. So income is reduced but a lower car price is a benefit. Competition policy stops two producers from merging. As a result we have two sets of overhead costs in the union where we could have only one. The stronger competition, however, gives a lower price, which is good. Finally, lowering the union's external tariff, so long as the number of producers is unaffected, only lowers price, and is unambiguously a gain.

The last case brings us back to a point that was mentioned in Chapter 2, that customs union issues are often discussed in models that imply that more liberal world trade would be generally beneficial, so that the tariffs in the model lack any direct justification.[4] Policy ranking in this type of model is made more difficult by the fact that strategic trade promotion can be a perfectly rational policy in a model with oligopolists, where an enterprise in one nation makes profits from sales to the residents of another nation. Note, however, that oligopolists will always makes profits on foreign sales, because they charge more than marginal cost. Therefore, other things being equal, car exports are a good thing for the nation precisely because they are non-competitive sales.

The ideal policy for the enterprising go-it-alone nation that can raise revenue with no costs from distortions or disincentives is to regulate car sales in the domestic market so that cars sell at marginal cost, to subsidise one domestic car producer's overheads and to allow the domestic producer a free hand to sell cars into foreign markets so as to maximise profits. The optimum involves anti-dumping, that is, selling more cheaply in the national market than in foreign markets.

To the two variables in the national welfare function correspond two separate motivations for trade and national production. Trade promotes competition, because it gives domestic buyers a greater choice of sellers, domestic and foreign. This tends to make prices lower and benefits national welfare. Sales to foreigners generate income that does not cancel out across domestic residents, as profits made by a national producer selling to domestic residents do. Such profits boost income of home residents and raise national welfare for any given car price.

There exists a motive for strategic trade promotion even in our simple model of oligopolies. To see this, imagine that a national car producer is just on the edge of going out of business for lack of net profit even when it is maximising. The oligopolist's calculation of profit and loss is no reliable answer to the issue of whether or not it is in the national interest that the plant should close. Two points may be noted, pulling in the opposite direction:

(1) the oligopolist counts profits gained by selling to national residents above marginal cost as part of its profit, while from the point of view of the nation this is just a transfer that cancels out across the nation;
(2) the price which will rule in the market if the domestic producer exits is discretely different from the current price. This upwards price jump has a social cost which the producer ignores.

So there is no general result that says that policy should support ailing but exporting producers, but that outcome could be encountered. There are obviously various ways of supporting the weak producer, and which are best is affected by the fact of oligopoly so that classical principles no longer apply. A lump-sum subsidy, independent of production, for example, is often recommended because it is less distorting than other kinds of intervention. Where foreign sales are involved, however, distortionary policies may not necessarily be a bad thing from the selfish national point of view, even if they are not the best of all policies.

Consider outright protection of the home market from imports, for example. In the well-known import-protection-as-export promotion model of Krugman[5] and others this can be an attractive policy because it allows the home producer to benefit from the decreasing marginal costs, which our model does not allow. Protecting the home market in the present model does nothing for exports. The now-monopolistic producer sells less in the domestic market than the previous total sales and the domestic price rises. Given that the domestic firm exists and operates, its exports levels are chosen independently of home sales. The constancy of marginal cost allows this separation. Thus protecting the home market neither helps nor harms exports.

The obvious implication of this argument is that strategic trade promotion could yet be very important if marginal costs fall with production level. Even in our simple model, however, protection can promote exports if it keeps a producer in business. It could even conceivably cause foreign producers to go out of business to the benefit of the home country. The conclusion may be that the literature has placed too much emphasis on decreasing marginal costs. These are important, no doubt, and the recognition of their importance is as old as Adam Smith.[6] Yet once the entry and exit of firms is made endogenous, import protection may amount to export promotion, even with constant marginal costs.

If knocking out foreign firms is a policy sponsored by the state, that would be the predatory behaviour of the type discussed earlier. To assess its importance one needs to leave the world of imagined models and to ask how often one encounters such cases in reality. An interesting example, often cited, is the international aircraft sales battle currently being waged between Boeing in particular on the one side and the European Airbus on the other. If this is a case in point, it is interesting to note that the spreading of overheads plays a far more important role than learning by doing or declining marginal costs. It is doubtful whether this is an example of the Krugman model or anything similar. Many of the overhead costs have already been paid and are irretrievably sunk. Governments are heavily involved and non-economic objectives abound. The export promotion mainly takes the form of sales subsidy. Private profit-maximizing behaviour can embrace taking a lower price in a foreign market than in the home market, but a sales subsidy makes sense only when there are falling marginal costs external to the individual producer.

To summarise briefly, large oligopolistic producers make significant differences in the context of customs union formation, and may provide intellectual justifications for either industrial or competition policy in a customs union context, and often for a cut in the rate of external protection when the union is established.

6.4 More general models and competition policy

It is surprising what a rich collection of insights can be obtained from a model that is simplified about as far as it is possible to simplify a model while permitting an examination of the effects of customs union formation. Even so, as fixed overhead costs are included in the model, profits can arise that will not be competed away by entry. Entry conditions and contestability of markets raise complex questions that are outside the scope of this volume.[7] To see that it is sound to suppose that incumbent firms will make profits, assume that overhead costs α are committed irreversibly, not necessarily forever, but at least for a long time.

To make sense of the inclusion of overhead costs α in a current cost function, they must be expressed as a flow charge per unit time. Imagine that the capital that the firm requires is hired via a long-term contract from which the firm cannot escape and which requires the payment of α per period. If another firm considers entry in the same country, it too must commit itself to pay α per period for a long time, when it knows that it will have to divide the market with the other firm for a long time. The resulting reduction of price in the home market and in foreign markets can easily mean that there is no net gain for the entering firm. The assumption that overhead costs involve long-term commitment has the effect that the war of attrition case examined in the literature, in which a firm enters a market to drive another producer out, will be of little practical importance.

Notice the difference between the question of the contestability of a market and the discussion of exit following the formation of a customs union earlier in this chapter. The point is that if the customs union is expected to be permanent, then a firm that makes a loss as a consequence of the customs union will eventually exit. If overhead expenses are fixed by long-term contract, it may take some time to exit, but exit will be the long-run outcome. With entry, however, the entrant has to consider whether to pay the overhead costs to enter, when their long-run nature mitigates against entry.

The presence of a car producer inside a country confers two distinct national benefits. First, it is a car producer in the world that might not be there – better still it is inside any tariff barrier. An extra producer implies downward pressure on car prices and this is to the benefit of consumers. From this point of view an extra producer anywhere is of some benefit. A producer inside the customs union is as good from the point of view of the consumer as a producer inside the home country, because it sets its sales at the same level as would a domestic producer. Secondly, if the car producer, now a national car producer, makes a profit, that constitutes an addition to national revenue.

As far as obtaining the profit is concerned, there is no need for the government to do anything. Private car producers, potential and actual, wish to make as much profit as possible. If there is just one national producer, then profit is maximised. If there are two or more producers, they will not maximise joint profit. In principle the government could tax the sales of the producers so as to drive them back to the same output as one firm would produce. Or it could operate such a slack competition policy that the firms were allowed, even encouraged, to merge to become one producer, when national profit from car production would increase. A slack national competition policy promotes car production profitability, anti-promotes exports and harms domestic consumers.

6.5 Conclusions

Our examination of the issues of imperfect competition and the customs union has only scratched the surface of a vast area. Even so, enough has been done to expose some important principles. First, customs unification, which does not result in the elimination of some producers, protects inside producers and promotes exports. In that sense it is trade diverting, although the term is not strictly appropriate because costs of production are the same everywhere. When producers are eliminated, either inside or outside the union, matters are more complex but the export promotion effect may well be reinforced. The benefit to consumers and the profit to the nation, in the sense of an element in the flow of national income, may go against each other and often do. But they can also work together, as happens when the multiplication of domestic producers does not harm total profit. Then profit does not fall and consumers benefit from lower prices. This is a particular but important sense in which the customs union is a movement in the direction of free trade. For one of the important effects of free trade is an increase in competition, which is always good for consumers. And that increase in competition, to the advantage of consumers, comes with a customs union and is one of its unambiguous benefits.

Appendix: Demonstrations and examples

A.1 *Market Shares and Prices*

We first derive the formula for price and market share precisely using the differential calculus. The producer's gross marginal revenue will be: $\frac{\partial p}{\partial x}x + p$, where the derivative shows the response of market price to the producer's own sales. Expanding the expression for gross marginal revenue we obtain:

$$\frac{\partial p}{\partial x}.x + p = \frac{\partial p}{\partial X}\frac{X}{p}\frac{x}{X}p + p = p\left(1 - \frac{s}{\epsilon}\right) \tag{6.9}$$

where ϵ, the elasticity of demand in the market; and s, the market share of the producer, are respectively defined by:

$$\epsilon = -\frac{\partial X}{\partial p}\frac{p}{X} \tag{6.10}$$

and:

$$s = \frac{x}{X} \tag{6.11}$$

The formula is the same as that derived in section 6.2 of the chapter.

A.2 *The customs union model*

To see more clearly how the simple three-symmetric-country three-producer customs union model works, we may solve an example as follows. Let each of the three countries have the same demand function for cars:

$$\log x = \log a - \epsilon \log p \tag{6.12}$$

where ϵ is the constant elasticity of demand for cars expressed as a positive number. We start with three symmetric countries each charging a tariff t in terms of food for the import of a unit of cars. Consider a producer in any country and his sales into a foreign market. Let $\hat{X}$ be the sales of other producers into the home market, and let x be the sales of the home producer into the home market. Then choosing x optimally, taking $\hat{X}$ as given, the producer chooses x and p to solve:

$$\text{Max } (p - c)x \tag{6.13}$$

subject to:

$$\log a - \epsilon \log p - \log(\hat{X} + x) > 0 \tag{6.14}$$

With λ the Lagrange multiplier on the constraint, this gives the first-order conditions:

$$p: \quad x - \lambda \frac{\epsilon}{p} = 0 \tag{6.15}$$

and

$$x: (p - c) - \lambda \frac{1}{\hat{X} + x} = 0 \tag{6.16}$$

These two first-order conditions together give:

$$\epsilon \frac{p - c}{p} = \frac{x}{\hat{X} + x} = \sigma \tag{6.17}$$

where σ is the market share of the home producer. An outside producer solves a very similar problem but now, as the tariff has to be taken into account, the problem is:

$$\text{Max } (p - c - t)x \tag{6.18}$$

subject to:

$$\log a - \epsilon \log p - \log(\hat{X} + x) > 0 \tag{6.19}$$

With $\hat{X}$ now being the sum of the local producer's sales and the other foreign producer's sales into the home market, and λ again the Lagrange multiplier on the constraint, which now takes a different value, this gives the first order conditions:

$$p: \quad x - \lambda \frac{\epsilon}{p} = 0 \tag{6.20}$$

and

$$x: (p - c - t) - \lambda \frac{1}{\hat{X} + x} = 0 \tag{6.21}$$

These two first-order conditions together give:

$$\epsilon \frac{p - c - t}{p} = \frac{x}{\hat{X} + x} = \frac{1 - \sigma}{2} \tag{6.22}$$

The last equation takes into account the fact that the share of an exporter in the symmetric case must be half the share not taken by the domestic seller – that is, $1 - \sigma$.

As the three shares must add up to 1, we have:

$$\epsilon \frac{p-c}{p} + 2\epsilon \frac{p-c-t}{p} = 1 \tag{6.23}$$

from which:

$$-\epsilon(3c+2t) = p(1-3\epsilon) \tag{6.24}$$

or:

$$p = \frac{\epsilon}{3\epsilon - 1}(3c+2t) \tag{6.25}$$

From the equation it may be seen that as ϵ goes to $\frac{1}{3}$ from above, the rate of cost markup, $\frac{p}{c+t}$, goes to infinity. This is the equivalent for the Nash oligopoly model of the everywhere unit elasticity of demand case for a monopolist. Note that with a constant elasticity of demand the price in each country increases linearly with the tariff.

Now consider the situation after two of the countries have formed a customs union, and with all three producers staying in business. In the outside country the market position is unchanged and market shares will be as before. This is true only because constant marginal production costs are being assumed. In each of the union countries there will now be two producers competing without paying the tariff and one outside producer paying the tariff. Otherwise the same equations for shares will hold. Asymmetry, however, now dictates that there will be two levels of car prices, one inside the union, denote it p, and another outside the union, which will be the same as the previous price level. Denoting the level of prices inside the union by p, which now takes a different value, the condition that market shares inside one of the union countries shall sum to unity is:

$$2\epsilon \frac{p-c}{p} + \epsilon \frac{p-c-t}{p} = 1 \tag{6.26}$$

This gives:

$$-\epsilon(3c+t) = p(1-3\epsilon) \tag{6.27}$$

or:

$$p = \frac{\epsilon}{3\epsilon - 1}(3c+t) \tag{6.28}$$

With a customs union the price inside the union falls by an amount:

$$\frac{\epsilon}{3\epsilon - 1}\, t \tag{6.29}$$

A.3 *A numerical example*

It is illuminating to compute the outcome for a numerical example. To this end, let a be 485 million. This seems like a large number, but note that it measures the market demand at a price of 1. Because c is chosen to equal 100, so that tariffs and markups are percentages of marginal costs, $p = 1$ corresponds to cars being sold at 1% of marginal cost, when a demand of 485 million cars is not ridiculous. The value of a places the demand function but is not itself of significance. Note that the log to the base e of 485 million is 20. Let $t = 25$ and $\epsilon = 2.0$. Then, prior to the formation of the customs union, price is:

$$p = \frac{2.0}{6.0 - 1}(300 + 50) = 140 \tag{6.30}$$

Whereas, after the formation of the union, price is:

$$p = \frac{2.0}{6.0 - 1}(300 + 25) = 130 \tag{6.31}$$

The fall in the price is 10, in conformity with the formula.

An observer of the economy depicted in the example might be disappointed by the effect of the customs union on the price of cars inside the union. A tariff on car imports of 25 units of food is reduced to zero, yet the price of a car in the dealer's showroom falls by only 10 units of food. In real life such pricing behaviour attracts criticism and talk of commercial conspiracy; yet we see that it follows from simple profit maximisation.

For the numerical example we may now compute market shares. For the home seller before the union is formed the share is:

$$\nu \frac{p - c}{p} = 2\frac{140 - 100}{140} = \frac{4}{7} \tag{6.32}$$

For each foreign seller before the union is formed the share is:

$$\nu \frac{p - c - t}{p} = 2\frac{140 - 100 - 25}{140} = \frac{1.5}{7} \tag{6.33}$$

We may now compute the profits made by each firm in the home market. At a price of 140, total demand X satisfies:

$$\log X = 20 - 2\log 140 = 10.12 \tag{6.34}$$

Then X = 24753 to the nearest integer. We may now compute the profits of the various sellers, not allowing for overheads, but taking into account the cost of paying the tariff for an outsider. The home producer takes four sevenths of sales, 14145. On each of those units it makes a profit of 40, giving a total profit of 565800. The outside sellers share the remainder of the market, selling 5304 units each and making a profit of 15 per unit, giving a total profit of 79560. As each producer is a home seller in one market and a foreign seller in two markets, the total operating profit of each producer is 565800 + 79560 + 79560 = 724920.

We may do similar calculations for the state of affairs that will apply after two of the countries form a union. After the union is formed the price inside it falls to 130 and we may recompute market share for an inside producer selling in a country inside the union as:

$$\nu\frac{p-c}{p} = 2\frac{130-100}{130} = \frac{6}{13} \tag{6.35}$$

While an outside seller has a share given by:

$$\nu\frac{p-c-t}{p} = 2\frac{130-100-25}{130} = \frac{1}{13} \tag{6.36}$$

Demand X satisfies:

$$\log X = 20 - 2\log 130 = 10.26 \tag{6.37}$$

Then X = 28708 to the nearest integer. Two inside producers each take six thirteenths of those sales, which is 13250, giving a profit of 397500 in each union market; 795000 for the two together. The outside seller shares the remainder of the market, selling 2208 units and making a profit of 5 per unit, giving a total profit of 11040.

When the union is in place the profitability of selling to the outside country is unaffected and that gives the home producer a profit of 79560 from those sales again. In each of the union markets the home producer enjoys a market share of $\frac{6}{13}$. Adding twice the profit from inside union sales to the profit from sales to the third country, we end up with a total operating profit of 795000 + 79560 =874560. With the customs union, profit for inside the union car producers has risen from 724920 to 874560. Yet the car price has fallen inside the union. The gain to the union is partly purchased at the expense of the third country. There car prices remain the same while exports and profits fall.

A.4 *The effect of a customs union on profitability*

In the case of this numerical example, the union has substantially increased profits for inside producers. Must that always happen? The answer is that it need not happen and that it depends on the values assumed. Consider the position of a monopolist in one of the markets. He chooses p and x to solve:

$$\text{Max } (p - c)x \tag{6.38}$$

subject to:

$$\log a - \epsilon \log p - \log(x) > 0 \tag{6.39}$$

With λ the Lagrange multiplier on the constraint, this gives the first-order conditions:

$$p: \; x - \lambda \frac{\epsilon}{p} = 0 \tag{6.40}$$

and

$$x: \; (p - c) - \lambda \frac{1}{x} = 0 \tag{6.41}$$

which together give:

$$\epsilon \frac{p - c}{p} - 1 = 0 \tag{6.42}$$

Or, in the case of the values of the example, $p = 200$. This gives a demand X that satisfies:

$$\log X = 20 - 2 \log 200 = 9.403 \tag{6.43}$$

and $X = 12129$. Operating profit is $12129 \times 100 = 1212900$.

These calculations assume each producer to be a monopolist in his own country, without giving any justification for the assumption. As a monopoly price of 200 emerges, however, it follows that a tariff of 100 will give sufficient protection to make it unattractive for the outside producer to sell in the home market. Therefore suppose that the tariff is initially 100 in all three countries. Then each producer makes the single-country monopoly operating profit, which is 1212900. Now let Arcadia and Bella – or any two of the countries – form a customs union, when they set tariffs on each other's imports at zero. Extra is still excluded and will not export to the union. Hence the equilibrium condition says that the shares of two non-tariff-paying producers shall sum to 1. That is:

$$2\epsilon \frac{p-c}{p} = 4\frac{p-100}{p} = 1 \tag{6.44}$$

From which it follows that $p = 133$. Demand is obtained from:

$$\log X = 20 - 2\log 133 = 10.22 \tag{6.45}$$

Then $X = 27427.5$. As each seller sells half the output in each market, profit is the same as if each seller sold all the output in his own market. The profit will be $27427.5 \times 33 = 905107.5$. Hence the formation of the customs union lowers profit for producers inside the union. It does this because it increases competition inside the union without providing the inside producers with a larger share of their home markets. As the share starts at 100%, it cannot be increased.

As has already been stated, it is not strictly correct to talk about trade creation or trade diversion in this simple model. The reason is this. As all countries have the same production costs, it does not matter, from the point of view of production efficiency, in which country cars are produced. We could easily alter that feature of the model by changing the numbers slightly; not enough to alter the structure of car production, but enough to introduce efficiency differences. Notice then that the type of case most likely to increase profits inside the union, and hence to produce the type of outcome shown, because no firms will be driven into bankruptcy, is also the type of case most likely to cause trade diversion. When Extra was exporting into the union countries, the union crowded out its exports when it was just as efficient as inside producers. It could have been a little more efficient and a similar result would have followed. Profit increases when trade is diverted.

In the second type of case with a very high tariff, Extra is in effect eliminated from consideration and the union promotes a lower price to consumers of cars. If there were differences in production costs, the union would favour the market share of the cheaper producer, which is trade creation. Yet this is the type of case in which the customs union can lower producers' profit. Profit can decrease when trade is created.

A.5 *The effect of the number of producers on profitability*

We may illustrate these results by recomputing the numerical example of section A.3, but now assuming two car producers in one of the union countries. The technique is the same for any similar example. Consider the home market, with two domestic competing producers, prior to the formation of the customs union. Four producers, two outside, two inside, divide the market.

$$2\epsilon\,\frac{p-c}{p} + 2\epsilon\,\frac{p-c-t}{p} = 1 \tag{6.46}$$

$$\frac{p-100}{p} + \frac{p-125}{p} = \frac{1}{4} \tag{6.47}$$

So that p = 128.6. Demand in the home market is 29350, with the market shares for respectively inside and outside producers equal to: insiders 0.445; outsiders 0.056. Then home producers sell 26122 on which they make an operating profit of 747089. Sales of the outside producer are 1644, yielding an operating profit of only 1644 × 3.6 = 5918. When there is a single producer in each country and no customs union, profit on domestic sales in one country is 565800 (see above). Two producers make a joint profit of 747089. Profit in the home market increases when there are two producers. This replicates a result noted by Tirole (1988) for a single market, that the merging of two oligopolists may decrease their combined profits.

In foreign markets before the customs union is formed, there are one insider and three outsiders:

$$\epsilon\,\frac{p-c}{p} + 3\epsilon\,\frac{p-c-t}{p} = 1 \tag{6.48}$$

Or,

$$\epsilon(p-c) + 3\epsilon(p-c-t) = p \tag{6.49}$$

From which:

$$p = \frac{\epsilon(4c+3t)}{4\epsilon - 1} = \frac{2(475)}{7} = 135.7 \tag{6.50}$$

Demand is 26341 and, as outsider's shares are 0.158, an outsider sells 4154 and makes a profit of 44448. Multiplied by four – two domestic firms and two outside markets – this gives a total national profit from foreign sales of 177792, and the combined profit for the two domestic producers from domestic and foreign sales together of 747089 + 177792 = 924881. This compares with the profit of 724920 that a single national producer made with no customs union. A slack competition policy, allowing one producer to monopolise the domestic market, is bad for profits. Profits on domestic sales fall, however. They must do so because the price has fallen, from 140 to 135.7, moving further away from the monopoly price. Profits on domestic sales are only an internal transfer; they neither add nor subtract from national welfare. So a slack competition policy, interpreted as laws that allow there to be only one national producer, entails a higher domestic car price. Add to this the point that two national producers combined make more profits on overseas sales than a single producer, and it will be clear that a weak competition policy does no good in this example.

After the customs union has been formed, the domestic market has three 'inside' sellers and one outsider. However, if we try to compute market shares for the domestic market using the same method as before, we find a negative market share for the outside producer. This means that the customs union cuts off car imports from outside the union. This can be confirmed by computing the shares of three inside sellers from:

$$3\epsilon \frac{p-c}{p} = 1 \tag{6.51}$$

Which implies $p = 120$. This confirms that the outside producer with costs of 100 plus the tariff of 25 that he will need to pay cannot compete inside the union.

Insiders' shares will be $\frac{1}{3}$ each. Demand is 33692. Profit on selling 13 of that is 224613. Two inside firms make that profit in each union market, giving a total profit of 898452. In the outside market the two producers again each sell 4154 units and make a profit of 44448. Twice over that represents 88896. Adding that to the profits on inside sales, we obtain a total profit of 987348. Table 6.1 shows the combined operating profits of national producers according to whether there is one or two, and according to whether there is or is not a customs union.

The table exhibits features specific to the numerical example. Profit is higher with a customs union than without one, and is higher for the country with two producers than for the country with one producer,

Table 6.1 Profits by number of producers and customs union

	No union	Union
One Producer	724920	874560
Two Producers	924881	987348

whether or not there is a customs union. It is obviously not generally the case that the more producers the better. As the number of producers in any country increases without limit the price in all countries tends to the cost of production. The tariff is added for an outside country that charges a tariff, but in any case all operating profit is extinguished. With overhead costs, the number of firms cannot increase beyond the point at which firms make only enough to cover overhead costs. At that point, profits must be falling with the number of producers.

Noting that we have not assumed marginal costs that vary with the scale of production, the assumption that underlies the Krugman import-protection-as-export-promotion model, we may take stock of the results that have been obtained with a constant marginal cost of production assumption. We have not considered changes in protection, simply understood, as such. Tariff rates have always been constant in the examples, although for the customs union they were cut to zero for intra-union trade. That has often meant that the customs union had no effect on market shares in the third country market. Again, when trade diversion is defined as Viner defined it, as a decrease in the efficiency of world production, the symmetrical model can only be silent, because world car production is equally efficient wherever the cars are produced.

This last conclusion is not robust. Let the three countries Arcadia, Bella and Extra have unit costs of car production equal to respectively 100, 90 and 70. With each country charging a tariff of 25, and many competitive producers in each country with the same unit costs, the Extra producers serve the home market and the market of Arcadia. If Arcadia and Bella form a customs union, Bella producers serve the Arcadia market, and production is diverted from a low-cost producer to a high-cost producer. That is standard Viner trade diversion. Now suppose that there is one producer in each country and we look at the Nash quantity-setting oligopoly solution.

Aside from the changed assumption concerning unit production costs, we keep to the other specifications of the numerical example; in particular, the elasticity of demand is 2 in each market, and all countries charge a tariff of 25 initially. Take the situation before the customs union is established. There are three different prices in the Nash solution, one for each market, denoted p^A, p^B and p^E. In Arcadia, the market shares, taking them in the order A, B, E, satisfy:

$$2\,\frac{p^{\mathrm{A}}-100}{p^{\mathrm{A}}}+2\,\frac{p^{\mathrm{A}}-90-25}{p^{\mathrm{A}}}+2\,\frac{p^{\mathrm{A}}-75-25}{p^{\mathrm{A}}}=1 \qquad (6.52)$$

which gives $p^A = 126$, and market shares for respectively A, B and E equal to: 0.4125, 0.175, 0.4125. In Bella, the market shares, taking them in the order A, B, E, satisfy:

$$2\,\frac{p^B - 100 - 25}{p^B} + 2\,\frac{p^B - 90}{p^B} + 2\,\frac{p^B - 75 - 25}{p^B} = 1 \qquad (6.53)$$

which gives $p^B = 126$ again, but now market shares for respectively A, B and E equal: 0.0159, 0.57, 0.4125. Finally, in Extra, the market shares, taking them again in the order A, B, E, satisfy:

$$2\,\frac{p^E - 100 - 25}{p^E} + 2\,\frac{p^E - 90 - 25}{p^E} + 2\,\frac{p^E - 75}{p^E} = 1 \qquad (6.54)$$

which gives $p^E = 126$, and market shares for respectively A, B and E equal to: 0.0159, 0.175, 0.8095.

If we now repeat the same calculations with the tariff for trade between Arcadia and Bella reduced to zero, we obtain the following findings. In Arcadia, the market shares satisfy:

$$2\,\frac{p^A - 100}{p^A} + 2\,\frac{p^A - 90}{p^A} + 2\,\frac{p^A - 75 - 25}{p^A} = 1 \qquad (6.55)$$

which gives $p^A = 116$, and market shares for respectively A, B and E equal to: 0.276, 0.4483, 0.276. In Bella, the market shares, taking them in the order A, B, E, satisfy:

$$2\,\frac{p^B - 100}{p^B} + 2\,\frac{p^B - 90}{p^B} + 2\,\frac{p^B - 75 - 25}{p^B} = 1 \qquad (6.56)$$

which gives $p^B = 116$ again, but now market shares for respectively A, B and E are: 0.276, 0.4483, 0.276. Finally, in Extra the market shares satisfy:

$$2\,\frac{p^E - 100 - 25}{p^E} + 2\,\frac{p^E - 90 - 25}{p^E} + 2\,\frac{p^E - 75}{p^E} = 1 \qquad (6.57)$$

which gives $p^E = 126$, the same as without the customs union, and market shares are again equal to: 0.0159, 0.175, 0.8095.

Table 6.2 shows the shares of the various national suppliers in each of the three markets. The rows show the three countries, the columns the three suppliers. In each cell the top figure shows the share of the supplier in the column in the market of the row before the customs union is formed. The lower figure shows the same share after the customs union has been established.

Table 6.2 Market shares with and without a customs union

A	B	E	
0.4125 0.276	0.175 0.4483	0.4125 0.276	A
0.0159 0.276	0.57 0.4483	0.4125 0.276	B
0.0159 0.0159	0.175 0.175	0.8095 0.8095	E

Table 6.3 Effect of a customs union on insiders' market shares

A	B	
0.702 0.381	0.298 0.619	A
0.0271 0.381	0.586 0.619	B

The oligopoly equivalent of the trade diversion exhibited in Viner's competitive model is clearly shown in the table. As Extra (Country E) has by far the lowest cost of production for a car, we may identify a decrease in Extra's share in the markets of Arcadia and Bella as a movement away from efficiency. If that movement away from efficiency results from the formation of a customs union, it makes entire sense to use the term trade diversion. In Table 6.2 we see that E's share of both A's and B's market falls from 41.25% to 27.6%. Surely this merits the term trade diversion.

When we apply a similar market share test to the effect of the customs union on B's share of A's market, where an increased share for B could be interpreted as an increase in efficiency, we seem to see an improvement because, with the customs union, B's share of A's market rises from 0.175 to 0.448. That looks like some trade creation to offset the trade diversion operating against E. That is not an enlightening way of looking at the effect of the customs union. If we instead examine B's share of A's and B's combined sales to the market of A we get a less biased measure of the trade creation effect. The effect of the customs union on A's and B's shares of their own markets is shown in Table 6.3.

The table is ambiguous on the question of trade creation between A and B. True the customs union has the effect that B's share of A's market increases, which is good, because B has a lower cost of production. Yet A's share of B's markets also increases. Despite A's low competitiveness, it gains in B's market as E's sales are pushed out by the customs union. On balance, the effect of the customs union is best described as trade diverting.

Lastly, consider competition policy. This may be interpreted most simply as a legal prohibition on two or more firms merging to make one producer. We have seen that when there are only two producers they can increase their profit only by merging. For they then become a monopolist, and the monopolist's profit is the maximum obtainable. When there are three producers, the minimum for a treatment of the customs union problem, it is no longer the case that a merger necessarily increases joint operating profits. It did not do so in the case of the example (see Table 6.1). That does not mean that a merger would be unprofitable even for the example case. By merging, the firms might avoid the duplication of overhead costs, which could easily more than offset a fall in joint operating costs. Yet consumers lose as a result of such a merger because the price increases. Also, the lower sales of domestic producers pull in imports. That helps to moderate the price increase, but with it comes a shift of profit abroad. If we imagine that all domestic profits are taxed away, so that their size has no effect on consumer welfare, it remains the case that a shift of profits abroad is to the benefit of off-shore residents and is like a cost to domestic residents. Hence, from the point of view of a single nation, a slack competition policy, which allows a merger to take place, has two costs and one benefit; which is not to say that the benefit may not exceed the two costs. The costs are a higher domestic car price and profit shifting abroad. The benefit is a saving in overhead costs that would otherwise be duplicated. If we adopt a union-wide view of welfare, imagining that transfers can offset distributional effects, then profit-shifting within the union is unimportant. Yet a slack competition policy shifts some profit outside the union, and that remains a cost.

A.6 *Solving the model with linear demand*

The computations of the model above employed the log-linear isoelastic demand function:

$$\log X = \log a - \epsilon \log p; \tag{6.58}$$

which has the advantage that the elasticity of demand, which figures in the standard expression for a market share, is a constant parameter of the demand function. Commonly used, however, because it makes the computations specially simple, is the linear demand function:

$$X = a - bp \tag{6.59}$$

where a is a new constant, not the same a as appeared in the log-linear function. Note that the elasticity of demand for the new function is:

$$-\frac{\partial X}{\partial p}\frac{p}{X} = \frac{bp}{a - bp} \tag{6.60}$$

which varies from 0 to infinity as p ranges from 0 to $\frac{a}{b}$, the price at which demand falls to zero. We keep the assumptions that $c = 100$, and that $t = 25$. With X denoting total demand, let sales of a particular seller be x when the total sales of all other sellers is $\hat{x}$. Hence $X = \hat{x} + x$.

Prior to the formation of the customs union, and with one producer in each country, the producer supplying his own market chooses x to maximise:

$$x[a - b(\hat{x} + x) - 100] \tag{6.61}$$

taking $\hat{x}$ as given. The first-order necessary condition for this maximisation is:

$$[a - b(\hat{x} + x) - 100] - bx = 0 \tag{6.62}$$

Or,

$$x = \frac{a - b_x - 100}{2b}. \tag{6.63}$$

The two outside producers solve a similar problem, except that cost is 125 rather than 100. This gives:

$$x = \frac{a - b_x - 125}{2b} \tag{6.64}$$

where now $\hat{x}$ takes a higher value, being the sales of one insider and one outsider, rather than the sales of two outsiders. Denoting the sales of the insider by x^{I} and the sales of an outsider by x^{O}, we derive two equations:

$$x^{\mathrm{I}} = \frac{a}{2b} - x^{\mathrm{O}} - \frac{50}{b} \tag{6.65}$$

$$x^{\mathrm{O}} = \frac{a - bx^{\mathrm{I}} - bx^{\mathrm{O}} - 125}{2b}. \tag{6.66}$$

These can be solved to yield:

$$x^{\mathrm{I}} = \frac{a - 50}{4b} \tag{6.67}$$

$$x^{\mathrm{O}} = \frac{a - 150}{4b} \tag{6.68}$$

This translates into an insider's market share:

$$\sigma^{\mathrm{I}} = \frac{a - 50}{3a - 350} \tag{6.69}$$

An outsider's share is:

$$\sigma^{\mathrm{O}} = \frac{a - 150}{3a - 350} \tag{6.70}$$

After the customs union is formed we can calculate shares as follows. The producer supplying his own market now has to compete with another inside producer and again chooses x to maximise:

$$x[a - b(\hat{x} + x) - 100] \tag{6.71}$$

taking $\hat{x}$ as given. This again leads to:

$$x = \frac{a - b\hat{x} - 100}{2b} \tag{6.72}$$

The one outside producer again solves a similar problem, and we obtain:

$$x = \frac{a - b\hat{x} - 125}{2b} \tag{6.73}$$

where again $\hat{x}$ takes a higher value, being the sales of two insiders. Again denoting the sales of an insider by x^{I} and the sales of an outsider by x^{O}, we derive equilibrium conditions for insiders and outsiders with a customs union as:

$$x^{\mathrm{I}} = \frac{a - bx^{\mathrm{I}} - bx^{\mathrm{O}} - 100}{2b} \tag{6.74}$$

$$x^{\mathrm{O}} = \frac{a - 2bx^{\mathrm{I}} - 125}{2b} \tag{6.75}$$

which can be solved to yield:

$$x^{\mathrm{I}} = \frac{a - 75}{4b} \tag{6.76}$$

$$x^{\mathrm{O}} = \frac{a - 175}{4b} \tag{6.77}$$

and this translates to market shares for respectively insiders and outsiders:

$$\sigma^{\mathrm{I}} = \frac{a - 75}{3a - 325} \tag{6.78}$$

$$\sigma^{\mathrm{O}} = \frac{a - 150}{3a - 325} \tag{6.79}$$

The result is qualitatively similar to the isoelastic case. The customs union causes Extra to lose market share in the markets of Arcadia and Bella. Thus σ^{O} falls from:

$$\frac{a - 150}{3a - 350} \tag{6.80}$$

to:

$$\frac{a - 150}{3a - 325} \tag{6.81}$$

and the second expression is obviously the smaller because it has the larger denominator.

Notes

1 For a view of the kind of results that may be obtained, see Brander and Spencer (1984), Grossman (1992), Helpman and Krugman (1985, 1989), Kierzkowski (1987) and Krugman (1986).
2 See also Winters (1991a), pp. 182–3.
3 For more intuition concerning this type of case, and for references to the literature, see Tirole (1988), 5.7.
4 See also Wonnacot and Wonnacot (1981).
5 See Krugman (1984).
6 See Adam Smith (1960), pp. 4–15.
7 A wide-ranging discussion will be found in Tirole (1988), Chapter 8.

CHAPTER 7

Currencies, exchange rate stabilisation and trade

7.1 The effects of exchange rate changes on trade

All the chapters until this one have been concerned with the real trade aspects of a customs union or a trade block. What relevance have different currencies, and the alterations in exchange rates that different currencies make possible, to the volume of real trade? Is there any connection between exchange rate variations and trade? The answer is that there certainly is such a connection. Indeed, one might say that that there is more than one connection between exchange rates and trade, or, equivalently, that the relationship that exists is complex and multi-faceted.

The most basic and simple argument says that different currencies in themselves constitute a barrier to trade, which would mean in this context that they would be a barrier to trade even if the exchange rates between them never changed. Despite its seeming implausibility, this argument has enjoyed considerable popularity. A favourite story of EC commissioner Leon Brittan has a tourist starting with £100 and changing it through all 12 EC currencies to end up with some pitiful sum, say £37. That would be the effect of 12 successive currency swops, each attracting a commission of 8%, certainly not an excessive assumption for the charge for small transactions in tourist exchanges. One may call this point, that changing currencies is costly, the *static cost* of currency differentiation – static because the cost is present even if exchange rates never alter. Then Leon Brittan's calculation and his wasted £63 would be an estimate, or rather an outlandishly inflated estimate, of the static costs of currency variety.

The slogan-like title of the book that reports a study originally undertaken by the Economic Research Division of the EC Commission is: *One Market: One Money.*[1] Is the sense of that slogan correct? Does one market, meaning here an effective customs union, require a single currency; and if so, why?

It is clear that the static costs of currency differentiation cannot be an important part of the case for the cruciality of a single currency. Plainly, for large traders and businesses the static costs are fairly unimportant. What matters is not exchange rates as such but rather the very real possibility that exchange rates may change. Do changes in exchange rates, or the possibility that exchange rates may change, generate a barrier to trade? The answer to this seemingly simple question has to be complex. The reason is that there are several distinct factors at work.

Many arguments for a single currency in Europe place their emphasis on the trade-discouraging effects of currency variation, as the static argument always does. Similarly, most theoretical writing argues that exchange rate variability discourages international trade.[2] Yet, historically a leading concern of policy makers has been that exchange rate variability will perversely stimulate trade to an excessive extent. Not only was such trade volatility seen as bad in terms of its resource allocation effects, it also pointed to the fear that it would undermine a liberal trade regime.[3] That is why, in the Bretton Woods design of the post-war policy environment, the liberal trade rules embodied in the GATT were seen as the natural twins and bedfellows of the exchange rate stabilisation enacted in the charter of the IMF. Only in the context of general open trade and currency stability, it was believed, would the individual country enjoy the incentive to forswear protection. Exchange rate volatility, on the other hand, would translate into large fluctuations in domestic prices of tradables in countries open to trade, and this would inevitably generate pressures to make the economy more closed to trade to avoid precisely that outcome.

A similar view influenced the policy thinking of the EC even from its foundation in the Treaty of Rome. Its authors recognised that there is a limit to how far treaty obligations can bind sovereign nations. Therefore it was important that the design of the EC common market should not be such that the rules agreed, on the one hand, and overbearing political pressure, on the other, would be opposed to each other. Those pressures might express themselves as governments not applying the free trade rules directly; through their conniving at irregular and illegal interferences with the rules by private parties; to their inability to stop such interferences.[4]

Given the existence of this general difficulty, the EC greatly aggravates the problem through the design and administration of its

Common Agricultural Policy (CAP). Imagine a group of countries open to free trade in agricultural goods, with the exchange rates between them subject to random and arbitrary shocks, having nothing to do with agriculture as such. Obviously such shocks will stimulate flows of agricultural goods. A 10% depreciation of one currency will make exports 10% more profitable to home holders of an agricultural stock than was previously the case, and will likewise make the imported product 10% cheaper to foreign buyers. With short-run demand and supply elasticities for agricultural goods both being low, however, the resulting flow of product from the country with the depreciated currency to other countries will soon raise the price of the good in the home currency and lower it in foreign markets until further flows are no longer profitable.

The CAP, however legislates price stabilisation, so that the benign adjustment process via price variation described cannot operate. Worse, with countries allowed to influence their 'green' exchange rates, and with all sellers, naturally, trying to sell 'into intervention' (i.e. to EC stocks) in the country and currency at which this is most profitable in domestic currency, the EC finds itself buying its stocks at the most unfavourable price. Giavazzi and Giovannini (1990) argue that this CAP problem was an important impetus behind the move towards currency stabilization in the EC. The additional costs of the CAP caused by the breakdown of exchange rate stability in Europe have serious consequences for the viability of the EC budget, because CAP disbursements account for well over half that budget.[5]

In this last case, two features are special. The manner in which the CAP fixes prices for agricultural goods and buys surplus production is not replicated even approximately for other types of goods and their markets. Also, the low elasticities of supply and demand for agricultural goods would mean that the automatic operation of the price system would offset many of the consequences of haphazard exchange rate fluctuation for domestic prices. What is the position if we look at markets in which no government price stabilisation system operates and where short-run elasticities of supply, and particularly of demand, may be much higher? Manufactured products will provide many cases in point.

With manufactured goods and traded services we encounter a new feature. If random exchange rate fluctuations were translated fully into price changes in foreign markets – if there was 100% exchange rate pass-through as the terminology has it[6] – then exchange rate movements would translate to huge alterations in the competitiveness of producers of similar products according to where they are located. This obviously could not happen with a simple undifferentiated product, such as nuts and bolts. Its producers have to price to the market (there is no exchange rate pass-through), and exchange rate movements can shift production around according to where costs converted to international value are lowest.

With a differentiated manufactured product, such as a motor car, the producer does not have price completely dictated by the market. For instance, the producer in a country with a high exchange rate can price foreign sales at the domestic price translated to a foreign currency price – 100% exchange rate pass-through. In that case, the high exchange rate will make the exported car expensive relative to similar models produced elsewhere. Yet that will not necessarily extinguish foreign sales. With a differentiated product there are always some buyers who like the product so much, by virtue of taste or habit, that they will buy it even when it is expensive. Even so, if producers did behave that way, random exchange rate movements would have seriously disruptive effects on trade in manufactured goods.

Broadly speaking, producers of manufactured goods stabilise the prices that they charge to foreign buyers against part at least of exchange rate movements. This is not for reasons shown in the model of Chapter 6. There, it is true, an exchange rate could be regarded as an increase in the cost of production, when the seller's share of a foreign market falls but the price remains fully competitive with that charged by other sellers. In that model, however, the product was in effect identical and undifferentiated between producers. Hence it was impossible for a seller to ask foreign buyers to absorb any part of his increased costs. When the home exchange rate appreciates, and the product is differentiated, however, the home seller could allow his price to rise above that charged for similar products. Sales would then be lost to other producers and the market share would be eroded.

Models of price stabilisation through exchange rate fluctuations argue that the preservation of market share, or the absolute scale of sales to a market, can be important to a seller, especially if overhead expenditures specific to a market are involved. An example would be the costs of establishing and maintaining a dealer network in a country. If that is allowed to go when the exchange rate makes sales to that market less attractive, the costs of re-establishing the same network from scratch will be massive. Yet the only effective way of keeping the network going through hard times will be to feed through it a sufficient volume of sales, which must be priced to sell. This by itself can imply the imperfect transmission of exchange rate changes into foreign prices. It may be that the relatively low importance of exports relative to the home market for many US producers accounts for a strong pass-through of the appreciation of the dollar in the 1980s into export prices, with the consequence that US exports suffered particularly. A comparison with Japan springs to mind, where exports are more important for many producers, and where a tendency to weak pass-through has often been noted.

All the arguments considered so far must be partial unless they are placed within a view of the nature of exchange rate shocks. Are these random and transitory events, or are they *innovations*, meaning that a movement of an exchange rate in one direction tends to persist unless reversed by another uncorrelated exchange rate shock. It seems at first that there would be no point in a producer absorbing an exchange rate innovation. If absorbing an exchange rate change is taken to mean reacting to it less than would be appropriate for a permanent change, then, almost by definition, it seems, an exchange rate innovation will not be absorbed. This view is too simple, however. The point is that there will be other reactions in the economy to an exchange rate innovation, some of which may be lagged. For instance, a 'permanent' (meaning uncorrelated with subsequent developments) appreciation in the home exchange rate may produce eventually a fall in the nominal prices of domestic inputs that will offset some of the loss in competitiveness caused by the exchange rate appreciation. Then some of the effects even of an exchange rate innovation will be temporary in character. In that case the same arguments as those considered above point to the producer absorbing part of the shock, to preserve market share, to sustain dealer networks, or for similar reasons.

Let us return the argument to the issue of whether fluctuations in exchange rates interfere with trade. Businessmen often complain about changes in exchange rates, and their answers to surveys (in Europe at least) usually reveal a preference for fixed exchange rates over variable exchange rates. Yet, from the analytical point of view, this is not always easy to understand. Exchange rate variability surely introduces uncertainty for producers exposed to international prices, which is most producers if indirect exposure is included. In the two following sections of this chapter, however, it is shown, first, that the relationship between price uncertainty and profitability is complex, and that it is certainly not the case that it is always bad for expected profit, although with strong risk aversion that might be irrelevant. Secondly, a change in an exchange rate could in principle help a producer and increase profitability. This would happen, for instance, if a producer is harmed by excessive costs of domestic inputs relative to a tradable output, when depreciation of the exchange rate would help that producer. This type of case, where the real exchange rate needs adjusting, is the subject of section 7.3.

The question of how profitability is affected by exchange rate changes is distinct from the issue of how trade flows respond to exchange rate volatility, but the answer is similar in its ambiguity. Section 7.2 examines the effect of exchange rate uncertainty on trade. The answer is again complex, depends on the particular assumptions made, and in any case is likely to be different for the short run and the long run.

7.2 The effect of exchange rate uncertainty on trade

The appendix shows some results on exchange rate uncertainty and trade more formally than in the present section. This allows a more intuitive and informal discussion here, secure in the knowledge that precise arguments in the appendix are available for the reader who needs a more formal treatment.

At first sight it seems obvious that a producer will dislike exchange rate variability, because exchange rate variability implies price variability, and surely producers dislike price variability. That may be so, but it cannot be because price variability as such is bad for profitability. On the contrary, variation of price holding its average value constant is good for expected profit.[7] To see why this is intuitively, consider a producer with unvarying input costs and an output price of 1.0; when the profit-maximising production level would be 100, costs would be 80 and profit would be 20. Now suppose that the output price will be 0.9 or 1.1, each value arising with probability $\frac{1}{2}$. If the producer still produces 100 units at each price, costs are unaffected, by assumption, and expected sales revenue is unchanged because the expected output price is still 1.0. Obviously the producer can do better than this, increasing production when the price is 1.1 and lowering it when the price is 0.9, and that adaptation would raise expected profit. In the appendix this result is made rigorous and generalised, and it is shown that it reflects the fact that the profit function is convex. So risk-neutral producers should welcome mean-preserving price variation because it increases expected profit. How is this result to be reconciled with the familiar argument of businessmen according to which exchange rate uncertainty (and presumably any price uncertainty) discourages investment?

One possibility is that the familiar argument is really quite partial. Producers voice their anxieties about exchange rate changes, and recall unhappy experiences in the past, neglecting to mention that sometimes exchange rate changes are favourable and that some past experiences were good. This would be similar to the situation with farmers, who notoriously always grumble about the weather, although it is plainly the case that the weather on average cannot be worse than average.

We also have to consider the implications of imperfect competition, because the theorem that states that producers gain in terms of expected profit from mean-preserving price variation assumes perfectly competitive producers. With imperfect competition, a change in an exchange rate shifts demand curves both for foreign and for domestic sales. The equivalent of a mean-preserving variation in price is a shift in the inverse demand curve, which gives the price in the market as a function of the quantity delivered to that market, with the shift being such that, for any quantity delivered, the expected price is the same. Then a similar argument to the one rehearsed above again shows that the producer benefits in terms of expected profit from random (interpreted as mean-preserving) changes in the exchange rate.

Finally, producers may be risk averse, in which case an increase in expected profit purchased at the cost of increased variability of profit may not be an improvement from the producer's point of view and investment in sectors subject to such risks may be discouraged. In fact it is highly plausible to assume that producers will be risk averse and will not wish to maximise the expected profit regardless of its variability. If random exchange rate movements add to the risk of exposure to trade, then exposure to trade will be discouraged. Notice how this result contrasts with the anxiety about the protection-promoting dangers of exchange rate variability discussed above. There the variability excited excessive trade flows. Now variability discourages trade.

The two arguments are in no way inconsistent, for one applies to the short run, the other to a longer run. Thus the flows of trade, particularly of agricultural goods, stimulated by fluctuations in exchange rates are mainly short run in character. It is true that one might make a case that the possibility of exchange rates fluctuating will discourage agriculture in the long term, if risk aversion predominates, or encourage it the long term, if the favourable effect of price fluctuation on expected profit predominates. Yet this is secondary to the main point, that short-run disturbances to trade movements may trigger irregular protection. On the other hand, the argument, which we have seen to require profit risk aversion, according to which exchange rate uncertainty discourages trade clearly applies to the direction of investment, whether it goes towards trade-orientated activities or not. And the direction of investment obviously has to do with long-run resource allocation.

Our argument must be compared with the findings of the important and masterly study of the effects of agricultural price stabilisation by Newbery and Stiglitz (1981), which the reader should consult for a wider-ranging discussion of the effects of price instability on allocation and welfare. There are some important differences, however, between the present exchange rate case and the agricultural price shocks discussed by Newbery and Stiglitz.

First, agriculture is treated by Newbery and Stiglitz, realistically enough, as an activity in which resources are first invested and for which the effects of price shocks come later. Hence there is no profit-function-convexity effect favourable to expected profitability. Secondly, producer profit risk aversion is given great weight, which obviously makes sense for farmers. Finally, price shocks are not treated as extraneous random, but mean-preserving, shocks. Rather, the effects of various demand and supply shifts are worked out through their general equilibrium implications for agricultural markets.

Even as a long-run argument to do with the direction of investment, the argument that has exchange rate uncertainty discouraging trade is quite special. It depicts an investor allocating his resources within one nation and choosing between activities vulnerable to exchange rate movements and activities not so vulnerable. If we allow investment to be internationally mobile, which is the appropriate assumption for the modern world, and certainly for a trade block, we reach different conclusions. Then, as elaborated in the appendix, exchange rate uncertainty encourages trade-promoting investment because it discourages the type of investment that is exposed too exclusively to the exchange risk of one country. The point is analogous to portfolio diversification theory. The risk-averse investor has an incentive to diversify, to place capital in numerous less than perfectly correlated economic activities. A car producer, for instance, might not be prudent to source all the parts and components of the car: engine, body panels, gear-box, etc., in one country because that would make profitability particularly vulnerable to a domestic exchange rate appreciation. It is entirely possible, therefore, that the circumstance that exchange rates may change will encourage more international movement of goods than would be the case without exchange rate uncertainty.

Sometimes exchange rate uncertainty seems to imply less trade, sometimes more. What are we to make of this? The answer must be that the extent of trade taken alone is no measure of what really matters, which is the improvement or a deterioration in the efficiency of world resource allocation. This is the same test as was applied with the customs union theory of Chapter 3. With ideas of protectionism and trade diversion in the air, it is too easy to think of more trade as a good, and a good under threat. In general, though, more trade can be good or bad, and, putting it simply, it is good if it takes production to low-cost sources and bad if it reflects more high-cost sourcing. That point illuminates the various examples of exchange rate fluctuation and uncertainty, and its consequences, that have been discussed. So, if random exchange rate movements provoke protectionism, that will surely be bad for efficient resource allocation. If they simply cause there to be flows of, say, agricultural goods that would not otherwise occur, the issue is more subtle. If the exchange rate movement reflects no underlying fundamentals but is a pure 'bubble', there can again be no serious case that resource allocation is improved. If we assume more plausibly that the exchange rate change reflects real changes in other parts of the economy, then the fact that it generates changes in the flows of agricultural goods having nothing to do with changes in agriculture does not mean that resources are being misallocated. If the home economy enjoys a resource boom, for example, caused by the discovery of natural gas, the exchange rate will appreciate and probably more agricultural goods will be imported or less exported. Irritating as this may be to the individual farmer whose activity is 'crowded out', it does not necessarily reflect resource misallocation in a general equilibrium sense. Similar ambiguities apply to the production diversification example, which showed a producer distributing the sources of inputs around different countries to diversify exchange rate exposure. Again, if we think of exchange rate changes as purely random noise, not reflecting economic fundamentals, then the production diversification will be purchased at the cost of sourcing some inputs at points with higher average costs, and that will be a decrease in average production efficiency. If, however, exchange rate changes reflect real shifts in the whole economy, but not necessarily in the sector under examination, then source diversification may correspond to real cost diversification, which cannot be counted as inefficient.

Many of the conclusions of the above discussion seem to depend on the ultimate cause of exchange rate movements, looking at the whole economy, not just at one sector. Those issues are examined more carefully in the two following sections of this chapter: the first looks at the role of exchange rate changes in improving global economic equilibrium, while the second examines the use of exchange rates as macroeconomic targets within a trade block.

7.3 The real exchange rate

The arguments of the previous section were unavoidably elaborate and they showed the effects of exchange rate changes to be subtle and to depend in detail upon the particular case considered. We have also, already, thrown doubt on the proposition that currency differentiation is a great problem for trade in its own right. In this section, rather than asking what harm fluctuations in exchange rates may or may not do, we turn the question round and ask instead what harm could fixed exchange rates do? Fixed exchange rates are discussed to focus the argument and bring points out clearly. Obviously, partially stabilised exchange rates, as with Europe's ERM during its successful operation of narrow bands for exchange rate fluctuation, raises similar issues. This is not to say that narrow bands for exchange rate variation, and strict fixed exchange rates, are close approximations to each other. On the contrary, the institutions required to implement the two are quite different, and narrow bands on the EMS model are inherently unstable according to Walters (1990).

On the face of things the advantages of fixed exchange rates seem obvious. Fixed exchange rates give a single currency for most practical purposes; they insulate the regions of a trade block against exchange rate disturbances, be they bubbles or temporary shocks; and they allow businesses to calculate the consequences of trade-exposed decisions with complete certainty as to rates of currency conversion. The trouble is that exchange rate stabilisation can fix only nominal exchange rates[8] and, although this is sometimes forgotten, it is not the nominal exchange rate about which traders ultimately care. Worse still, the exercise of stabilising nominal exchange rates can turn out to be positively inimical to stabilising or adjusting (whichever is appropriate) what does matter for economic equilibrium and the effective operation of the price system, which is real exchange rates.

The real exchange rate may be explained most easily for an economy in which all goods are either wholly tradable, so that their prices must compete directly with those of closely similar goods produced in other countries, or completely non-tradable, where the latter category includes domestic factors of production, especially labour. Then the real exchange rate that best serves our present purposes is the ratio of the price of non-tradables (an index number if necessary) to the price of tradables. This number measures how profitable it is to convert domestic goods into international goods (a low real exchange rate makes it more profitable), or to substitute imported goods for similar domestic goods (a low real exchange rate makes that less attractive). Notice that an increase in the productivity of all non-tradables and an equivalent appreciation of the real exchange rate offset each other exactly. Hence changes in real exchange rates affect trade and trade performance, and thus national economic balance, in just the way that changes in nominal exchange rates are often supposed to do. The difference between the two cases, however is crucial. The ultimate effects of changes in nominal exchange rates are intricate and uncertain, partly because exchange rate changes trigger complex and unpredictable effects on domestic prices. It is notorious, for instance, that the beneficial effects of a required currency devaluation may be dissipated via domestic inflation. That is only to say that a nominal devaluation may not translate to a lasting real exchange rate depreciation.

The real exchange rate defined as the ratio of the price of non-tradables to the price of tradables cannot be measured directly. Hence many writers define the real exchange rate as the relative price of two currencies corrected for their purchasing power given the price levels in the two countries.[9] Fortunately the present argument makes sense with either interpretation of the real exchange rate.

For the ideal operation of a trade block, the real exchange rates of individual countries should take values such that the distribution of production between them correctly reflects real comparative advantages. If, for whatever reason, real exchange rates depart from these values, one would hope for an adjustment of these exchange rates in the right direction. How is this to be achieved? For the purpose of answering this question ignore the case of the country that faces acute difficulties in adjusting its real exchange rate to reach equilibrium. That would happen, for example, in the case of a country with chronic government over-spending that needs to be moderated to make the achievement of equilibrium possible. When equilibrium can be achieved, it can typically, in principle, be attained by more than one route. Suppose that the real exchange rate is over-valued, discouraging exports and tending to produce a current account deficit. Perhaps the consequence will be that macroeconomic policy will be applied to deflate the economy and there will be unemployment of some factors.

One solution to this difficulty would be for domestic prices of non-tradables to fall (think of a fall in wage rates, or the moderation of wage rises in an inflationary situation, as an example of such a response). These price adjustments depreciate the real exchange rate and provide one route out of real exchange rate maladjustment. An alternative path would take the form of a depreciation of the nominal exchange rate. This would raise the domestic price of tradables, hence depreciating the real exchange rate again.[10] If the first route to adjustment was always open and easy to use, there would be no need to worry about the second route, which involves nominal exchange rate adjustment. Unfortunately, however, nominal domestic price adjustment, which may take the form of inflation moderation, is difficult and costly to achieve. How far these problems tend to arise will depend upon how close the regions or countries in the currency union are in the relevant sense, that is how far they are similarly affected by shocks and by trends in their economic development. Alternatively, different regions may be able to adapt to divergent developments under a common currency by wage and other domestic price adjustment. If any or all of these vital conditions are satisfied, the regions concerned constitute an optimum currency area.[11] Current high unemployment levels in Europe, which partly reflect the costly process of grinding down high inflation rates in several countries, suggest that Europe does not enjoy the status of an optimum currency area.

That is, and has always been, right back to Bretton Woods and even to the gold standard, the downside of nominal exchange rate stability. It throws all the burdens of adjustment onto domestic price flexibility. Of course this is even more acutely the case with a single currency. An optimistic view says that nominal exchange rate fixity positively encourages domestic price flexibility. That would happen, for instance, if trade unions' knowledge that exchange rate depreciation would not come to their rescue if they set wages too high, led them to moderate wage demands. This may happen, but it is not obvious that it will happen to a sufficient degree, especially not in Europe where price flexibility is much less than will often be required.[12] Indeed the EC from its foundation has conceived of a Europe in which some countries or regions will engage in what might be called assisted adjustment, effected by centrally funded transfers. In principle these transfers should allow input prices to adjust all the way without requiring their owners to take the full cut on the income side.[13]

To summarise the argument of this section, a trade block needs some way of regulating the coexistence of its different regions or nations and organising their mutual adjustment to various developments in technology, tastes and other factors. In that context, exchange rate fixity is convenient in some ways. It suppresses certain kinds of shock that disrupt only trade and cause resource misallocation, it avoids some provocations to free trade, and it may even promote domestic price flexibility. On the other hand, the same institution denies the participating units the facility of easy adjustment via exchange rate changes. That facility may encourage inflationary tendencies, but it may also allow high-inflation units to survive with less catastrophic macroeconomic consequences. A trade block does not need a single currency; it may find one convenient, but it may not be able to afford that luxury. The relation between the control of inflation and exchange rate stabilisation is briefly discussed in the next section.

7.4 The exchange rate as policy target and anti-inflation anchor

In the past, countries whose price levels inflated too rapidly relative to the rest of the world suffered from balance of payments problems, when they either had to alter macroeconomic policy variables to moderate inflation, or had to allow the exchange rate to depreciate. By inhibiting the second of the two alternatives, exchange rate stabilisation always implies some control of inflation. Specifically, it controls inflation relative to the world or block inflation rate. That is why, to be fully effective as a macroeconomic regulator, exchange rate stabilisation requires an anchor, a low-inflation currency that will tie down the family of stabilised currencies to low inflation. Until the late 1960s that anchor function was provided by the US dollar in a world-wide Bretton Woods currency system. In EC Europe a similar part has been played by the Deutschemark.

As expectations have become more important, governments have needed not just to do right, but also to be expected to do right. Hence the issue of credibility has become central to concerns about macroeconomic policy. In the EC, several governments – the Spanish government is a leading example – have used commitment to the ERM rules for their exchange rates to lock themselves into low-inflation credibility. In effect they attempted to make their macroeconomic policy exogenous by surrendering it to the overbearing requirements of exchange rate management.

We now arrive at a paradox. If the stability of the exchange rate becomes completely credible, then the home currency becomes a near perfect substitute as far as portfolio holders are concerned for any other currency in the group. In that case foreign investors come to care less about inflation, which they no longer associate with dangers of devaluation. The penalty for inflation now falls on the home country, forcing it to suffer a loss of competitiveness and higher unemployment. But if it tries to lower inflation by means of a tight money policy, capital will flow into the country and push up the exchange rate, possibly undermining the very instrument, exchange rate stabilisation, on which the policy was founded. Hence credible commitment to exchange rate stability is not necessarily an effective anti-inflation device and it may contain the seeds of its own downfall.[14]

If exchange rates are subverted to the purpose of macroeconomic credibility, it is obvious that they cannot serve the end of efficient microeconomic allocation. Indeed the two aims can easily end up in direct opposition. This happens when real exchange rates get out of line, while nominal stability for the end of credibility, or so-called uncertainty reduction, prohibits a change in the exchange rate. In fact, if we focus on the promotion of efficient trade it is doubtful whether exchange rate flexibility is of much import. The EC became a block and intra-block trade flourished while exchange rates were not stabilised. Similarly, trade flourished between the USA and Canada while the Canadian dollar floated. It is true that runaway inflation is bad for trade, mainly because reform is eventually unavoidable, which typically disrupts the allocation of resources, e.g. because of unemployment results.

For the EC, two general points may be made:

(1) In so far as inflation moderation was achieved in Europe via the EMS, particularly for the countries in the narrow 6.5% bands, this was not what the EMS was designed for. In a Europe with all countries inflating rapidly the EMS would have done nothing for inflation moderation. The policy worked because of the particular and asymmetric position of Germany and the strong dislike of inflation on the part of the Bundesbank. Yet the Bundesbank was not willing to take on the role of a European central bank but addressed its policy mainly to the domestic German situation.

(2) The use of nominal exchange rate stabilisation as an anti-inflation measure affected and corrupted the EMS by making it more rigid. The reason is that, once countries had tied their anti-inflation banners onto their exchange rates, they could no longer use nominal exchange rate adjustment to respond to shocks, as the EMS allows.

This awkwardness turned into a fatal flaw with the shock of German reunification.

7.5 Concluding remarks on exchange rates

The view that says that exchange rate stabilisation, or a common currency, is essential to a customs union has not found much support from our analysis. The thirty-year-old theory of the optimum currency area says that a group of countries benefit from having a common currency if they satisfy some essential properties, but does not promise massive gains from there being a common currency, still less from the moderation of exchange rate fluctuations.

The argument that says that exchange rate stability promotes trade is quite misleading unless amplified and qualified. First, promoting trade, meaning putting in place institutions that increase the level of trade, is not the same as doing good. We have seen that exchange rate uncertainty can increase the level of trade and in more than one way. It may draw low-risk-aversion investment into exchange rate exposed activities because mean-preserving exchange rate fluctuation increases expected profitability. It may also promote international diversification of sourcing by risk-averse decision makers. That is an example of trade promotion that is not an improvement in block resource allocation.

Those arguments are microeconomic in character. Not all the arguments for a single currency, say in Europe, have been microeconomic. The macroeconomic case is essentially an advocacy of macroeconomic coordination, which is always a good thing if it can be made to work, although not necessarily hugely valuable. Macroeconomic policy coordination is potentially more valuable the more the coordinating countries trade and the more their uncoordinated policies differ from what they would be with coordination. Not all these features are necessarily associated with a trade block. While high intra-block trade should be a feature of a successful block, policy coordination does not need membership of a trade block and was originally proposed for the policies of fully independent nations.

Recent European experience has added exchange rate management, in the direction of stability, as a badge of anti-inflation credibility. At its base this had little to do with the trade block as such. That claim may seem surprising, for surely the EMS played an essential role? No: the Deutschemark played an essential role, because it provided an anchor to which a country seeking anti-inflation credibility could tie its currency. EMS membership was a way of tying to the Deutschemark, but for two years Britain showed in its exchange rate management that EMS membership was not an essential means, by stabilising its exchange rate with the Deutschemark while being outside the EMS.

Appendix: Exchange rate uncertainty and trade

This appendix shows some results on exchange rate uncertainty and trade in a framework more formal than the relaxed discussion of the main text of the chapter. Leaving aside problems of trade imbalance and macroeconomic adjustment, the text discussion focused on the issue of how exchange rate volatility would affect the trade or anti-trade bias of investment decisions. Here two simple models demonstrate the main points discussed.

Model 1
The investor has to decide how much of a resource to invest in a trade-biased project, defined as one for which there is a high level of price uncertainty relative to the alternative project that would otherwise absorb the resource, taken to enjoy price certainty for the sake of simplicity. The projects are in every other respect equivalent; hence their profit functions satisfy:

$$\Pi^1(\bar{p}) = \Pi^2(\bar{p}) \tag{7.1}$$

where $\Pi^i(p)$ is the profit function with respectively trade bias ($i = 1$) and anti-trade bias ($i = 2$), and $\bar{p}$ are mean prices. Extreme anti-trade bias in this context means that $\Pi^2(p)$ is unaffected by the exchange-rate-induced price variations that we are considering and its value can be considered as a constant. $\Pi^2(p)$ is on the other hand affected by price variations. Because the profit function is convex, mean-preserving price variation raises expected profit. Hence, if only expected profit mattered, as would be the case with risk-neutral producers, resources would be shifted towards trade-biased projects.

The next result uses a production model analogous to the portfolio diversification model.

Model 2
The investor has to distribute a fixed amount of a resource (capital) between n different projects, which are differentially affected by exchange-rate-induced price variations. More projects equals more trade. Different national sourcing for car components would serve as an example. Let the investor have capital c^0 and allocate c^i to project i.

Then:

$$\sum_{1}^{n} c^i = c^0 \tag{7.2}$$

and the expected value of the sum of the investments is:

$$E\left[\sum_{1}^{n} \Pi^i(p, c^i)\right] = \sum_{1}^{n} \overline{\Pi}^i \geq \sum_{1}^{n} \Pi^i(\overline{p}, c^i) \tag{7.3}$$

where E is the expectation operator, $\Pi^i(p, c^i)$ is the profit function for project i when investment allocated to it is c^i, $\overline{\Pi}^i$ is its expectation, and $\overline{p}$ is $E(p)$, the expectation of the price vector. The inequality above again uses the fact that, because the profit function is convex, a mean-preserving price variation raises expected profit.

Now the variance of total profit is:

$$E\sum_{i=1}^{n}\sum_{j=1}^{n}\left[\Pi^i(p, c^i) - \overline{\Pi}^i\right]\left[\Pi^j(p, c^j) - \overline{\Pi}^j\right] \tag{7.4}$$

As usual, the risk-averse investor has an incentive to diversify, to place capital in numerous less than perfectly correlated investments. If the variance–covariance matrix of the Π^i values were to be diagonal, indicating independence of the performance of the different investments, diversification would be indicated because the variance of the sum of n independent parts is smaller than the variance of the one part of the same total size. If, further, covariances are negative, showing a tendency for investments to perform well just when others perform badly, the case for diversification is powerfully reinforced.

The two models arrive at somewhat different conclusions concerning the effect of random exchange rate fluctuations on the volume of trade. Model 1 seems to say that exchange rate fluctuation encourages activities exposed to its effects. This, however, is an outcome dependent on expected profit playing the leading role (i.e. on investors having a low degree of profit risk aversion) combined with the convexity of the profit function property noted above. Risk aversion with regard to the outcome of investments works in the opposite direction, for this naturally makes investments exposed to random exchange risks less attractive, and encourages an autarkic orientation of production. In the case of Model 2, risk aversion promotes (possibly over-promotes) trade, simply because it encourages diversification, especially for negatively correlated risks.

Notes

1 For the full title and the reference see Emerson et al. (1992).
2 See, for instance, Gagon (1993).
3 The point is mentioned by Bhagwati (1992) and also by Krugman (1989).
4 Examples would be as follows: government officials refusing registration of legally imported cars would be a direct government breach of the rules; instructing the police not to act against farmers blockading a port to inhibit imports would be connivance; and lacking the power to stop such illegal actions would be the third case. Obviously clear dividing lines can be difficult to draw.
5 On EC finance, see Shackleton (1990).
6 See Dixit (1989) and Froot and Klemperer (1988).
7 The assumption that exchange rates are as likely to go up as down, which is a feature of the mean-preserving assumption, is natural if expectations concerning the value of exchange rates are rational (i.e. unbiased with respect to the mean).
8 At least that is true of systems of exchange rate stabilisation that operate on the nominal exchange rate. Important though these are (Bretton Woods and the EMS are two examples) mild stabilisation of what are essentially real exchange rates has been proposed. See Williamson (1983).
9 For a clear explanation of the distinction, see Ethier (1988), pp. 397–8. See also Caves, Frankel and Jones (1993), pp. 396-401, and Winters (1991a), p. 249.
10 The consequences for the real domestic monetary supply will typically be different. We assume that the domestic money supply is adjusted to offset such differences.
11 See Kenen (1969) and Mundell (1961).
12 The argument has been extensively developed and expounded elsewhere. See Bean (1992), Eichengreen (1990) and Feldstein (1992).
13 The type of local input subsidy described was not what the EC opted for; it instead selected infrastructure subsidy on the apparent assumption that this would moderate the need for local price flexibility. There is no evidence that this view was correct.
14 See Walters (1990).

CHAPTER 8

Conclusions

Results already discussed allow us to counter what may be called second-bestism. A should protect because B is protecting, to avoid the distortion that would arise if A liberalised alone. Every distortion justifies a similar distortion: think of an optimum tariff answered by an optimal tariff response. The popular version of second-bestism is the so-called level playing field argument, which says that freer trade is fine provided that no country is doing anything to distort world trade. One thing that a trading block provides is the same as the original GATT provided – reciprocity. Although theoretical models may show unilateral free trade to be beneficial, most countries would mostly like the benefits of free trade access to other markets while reserving for themselves the right to protect their own markets selectively against imports. In other words, they would like to free-ride on free trade arrangements.

In the language of game theory, the GATT, and similar agreements, may be seen as a way of implementing a cooperative solution to a game in which strict adherence to free trade principles is not maximising for individual countries. Treaty rules may be seen as a mechanism for increasing the cost of defection from liberal trade cooperation. Protection that would be an irritation were there no formal agreement is turned into a provocation that cannot be ignored when it crosses legally established lines. The weakening of the GATT may then be interpreted almost as a cooperative strategy of the large countries to establish new boundary lines without upsetting the entire structure. This would include the establishment of, and GATT connivance with, the multi-fibre agreement, or the use of import quotas.

If the weakening of the GATT has gone too far, why should that promote the establishment of trading blocks, rather than producing among the leading trading nations a wish to reform GATT in order to re-establish its effectiveness? Both processes have been observed but, for Europe at least, the momentum towards the trade block seems to be the stronger force. If trading blocks are substitutes for the GATT, are they not inferior second-best substitutes? Trade theory says that they may not be too seriously inferior; that is a matter of block design, as has been seen.

In explaining why the not-seriously-inferior should be preferred to the best, however, international politics will play the largest role. While the world has become smaller in terms of transport costs and communication, it has fragmented to some extent in terms of the horizons of its peoples. The end of the Cold War has greatly accelerated this process, which was under way in any case. The interplay between politics and economics in the formation of the trade block is fascinating. Where politics typically provides the motivation, economic integration is often the means. It was thus with the original European Communities: politics drove the movement towards closer union but an economic integration is what resulted.

Economic theory may claim that gains from trade are what maximise the benefits from block formation. In truth, however, a block is not a set of regulations: it is a cooperative administrative apparatus; it is even an example of the game theorist's cooperative agreement. If it is not to be dominated by one large nation, it may demand an effective coalition and combination of interests. That is easier where common histories are shared and where a similar culture facilitates communication and the establishment of trust.

The political, cultural, or simple geographic, affinities that permit a trade block to be formed are lubricating oil to the process of block formation. Yet the same forces may stand in the way of globalising free trade. The arguments of earlier chapters have proved that block gains from trade do not need to be purchased at the expense of global gains from trade; that local free trade and global free trade are complements, not substitutes. These are theorems in the economics of resource allocation that may not translate to the realities of team operations. Any trade block, but especially the non-hegemonic type, has to coordinate diverse, and sometimes strongly opposed, internal interests between nations or regions or factors. While we have seen that mechanisms exist to facilitate that process, they are not easy and they may not be used. In that case an apparently attractive way of reconciling diverse internal interests is to buy them off at the expense of outsiders. Thus a trade block may find it convenient to become more protectionist towards the outside world, say by increasing terms-of-trade-improving tariff levels, not because the Kemp–Wan theorem is incorrect, but because that beggar-my-neighbour route will increase the rents available inside the block to be dispersed to pay off offended interest groups.

The right answer in theory to beggar-my-neighbour tendencies is negotiated international agreements to desist from such activities, and that, in short, is what the GATT delivered to the post-war world. Yet the GATT has lost effectiveness and it needs reform. Various ideas are being discussed, in the Uruguay Round negotiations and elsewhere. Major problems, however, stand in the way of an ideal reform. Deficiencies in the original treaty could be repaired, but the complexity of modern techniques of trade management make it hard to design a system for policing modern interblock trade. There was conflict between great powers over the form and methods of the original GATT when that was negotiated. Yet in the climate of a war-torn world looking forward to peace and reconstruction, and with the powerful USA playing a leading role in the negotiations, most of the difficulties could be overcome. Today's world is more symmetric, with economic and political power more dispersed. And trade blocks, or large nations, exist and are leading negotiators. These have put in place, or plan to put into place, frameworks within which their own internal trade will be regulated. Can a legal structure for the regulation of inter-block trade be built around and over the arrangements that blocks have made for the conduct of their internal trade? One could even envisage a two-tier world trading system with very liberal trade within blocks, and less liberal, but still law-regulated, trade between blocks.

A danger is that we will not get to that unless the GATT is reformed, because otherwise its weaknesses will cause it to be marginalised. So a new treaty is needed. Ideally, this time it should establish a more substantial administration than the present GATT process, and even be provided with its own treaty-empowered International Trade Court (ITC) for the arbitration and legislative settlement of disputes. The principle of a general requirement of transparency would be admitted, implying that restrictive trade agreements, such as voluntary export restraints, should be registered with the new administration and should be required to conform to some basic principles. The ITC would have the power to grant to countries specific periods to adjust to embarrassing import penetration, and would be empowered to penalise countries for the grossest breaches of trade rules. In principle, all goods moving in trade, including agricultural goods, services, intellectual property rights, etc., should be covered. And the new treaty would face the issue of dumping, and the unilateral imposition of counter-dumping duties, head on. Mainly, only ITC would have the power to impose anti-dumping duties or quotas, beyond a short period of time, and, by virtue of that power, it would be able to prohibit the most outlandish anti-dumping and dumping acts; including bully-boy use of anti-dumping actions against small politically weak nations (such as Hong Kong) and EC foodstuffs dumping.

Unfortunately, the world is almost certainly not in the mood for such a radical extension and consolidation of the GATT. Perhaps the best that can be hoped for realistically is the prohibition of the worst trade torts over a broad up-to-date range of goods and services reflecting the range and weightings of goods and services in today's trade. That does not have to mean that outside those limits inter-block trade will inevitably deteriorate into a jungle, because large trade actors will be able to use their weight to discourage too much protection being aimed at them. A balance of trade terror may not be an encouraging prospect for the world as it enters the third millennium, but it may prove to be stable, as the balance of nuclear terror did during the Cold War.

Despite the massive and evident problems for international trade in the modern world, trading blocks have come into being and are being developed and extended. The lesson may be that the entire world is too large an area on which to establish the most free trade that is possible. To put it another way, the simple idea that customs unions or free trade areas are a good step in the right direction may not be exactly right as economic theory, for it depends on union design, as we have seen, but it is entirely right as a description of political administrative feasibility. If the trading block works as an institution with good generation and survival performance, it might plausibly be made the basis for the design of the world trading system. One might even wish to promote the organisation of countries not currently included in a trading block, especially numerous developing countries, either into new, probably regional, trading blocks in their own right, or into satellite relationships with the existing major trading blocks.

That will not dispose of the world trade problem, because trade between blocks is very important. For the outside world to be denied the benefits of Japanese design and production skills, or to lose the advantages of US climatic endowment, land abundance and agro-technique, where food is concerned, and so on, would be heavy costs. Once, however, the trading block is accepted, not as a sinister development that we would really like to stamp on, but as part of the right answer, we can then turn our attention to rules for inter-block trade. The objectives of these rules would need to be less ambitious than would be appropriate for rules designed to regulate the whole of world trade. Locally, within blocks, self-policing would regulate trade, and we would be looking only for rules to encourage inter-block trade and to prohibit policies excessively harmful to those outside the block. In principle this route offers gains to all countries and to all members of blocks. If those benefits are not realised, it will not be because the technical problems are overwhelming, although they are far from being trivial. It will be because politicians and their electors have lost faith in the benefits of global free trade and converted to a mercantilism for which they will pay a high price in terms of lost prosperity and economic harmony.

REFERENCES

Balassa, B. (1975), 'Trade creation and diversion in the European common market', in B. Balassa, ed., *European Economic Integration*, Amsterdam: North-Holland.

Baldwin, R. E. and J. E. Richardson, eds (1988), *Issues in the Uruguay Round*, NBER Conference Report, Cambridge, Mass.: NBER.

Baldwin, R. E. and J. E. Richardson, eds (1991), *The Uruguay Round and Beyond: Problems and Prospects*, NBER Conference Report, Cambridge, Mass.: NBER.

Bean, C. (1992), 'Economic and Monetary Union in Europe', *Journal of Economic Perspectives*, Vol. 6, 4, 31-52.

Bhagwati, J. (1991), *The World Trading System at Risk*, Hemel Hempstead, Herts: Harvester Wheatsheaf.

Bhagwati, J. (1992), 'The threats to the world trading system', *The World Economy*, Vol. 15, 4, 443–56.

Bhagwati, J. and H. T. Patrick, eds (1990), *Aggressive Unilateralism*, Hemel Hempstead, Herts.: Harvester Wheatsheaf.

Bhagwati, J. and T. N. Srinivasan (1993), 'Trade and the environment: Does environmental diversity detract from the case for free trade?', paper prepared for the Ford-Foundation-financed project on *Fair Trade and Harmonization.*

Bliss, C. and J. de Macedo, eds (1990), *Unity with Diversity: The European Community's Southern Frontier*, Cambridge: Cambridge University Press.

Brander, J. and B. Spencer (1984), 'Tariff protection and imperfect competition', in H. Kierzkowski, ed., *Monopolistic Competition and International Trade*, Oxford: Clarendon Press.

Caves, R. E., J. A. Frankel and R. W. Jones (1993), *World Trade and Payments*, 6th edition, New York: HarperCollins.

Cooper, C. A. and B. F. Massell (1965), 'A new look at customs union theory', *Economic Journal*, Vol. 75, 742–7.

Corden, W. M. (1972), 'Economies of scale and customs union theory', *Journal of Political Economy*, Vol. 80, 465–75.

Corden, W. M. (1974), *Trade Policy and Economic Welfare*, Oxford: Clarendon Press.

Corden, W. M. (1984), 'Normative theory of international trade', Ch. 2 in R. W. Jones and P. B. Kenen, eds, *Handbook of International Economics*, Amsterdam: North-Holland.

Curzon-Price, Victoria (1992), 'New institutional developments in GATT', *Minnesota Journal of Global Trade*, Vol. 1, 1, 87–110.

Dasgupta, P. S. and J. E. Stiglitz (1974), 'Benefit–cost analysis and trade policies', *Journal of Political Economy*, Vol. 82, 1–33.

de Melo, J. and A. Panagariya (1993), *New Dimensions in Regional Integration*, CEPR, Cambridge: Cambridge University Press.

Diamond, P. A. and J. A. Mirrlees (1971), 'Optimal taxation and public production', *American Economic Review*, Vol. 61, 8–27, 261–78.

Dixit, A. K. (1988), 'Optimal trade and industrial policies for the US automobile industry', in R. Feenstra, ed., *Empirical Methods for International Trade*, Cambridge, Mass.: MIT Press.

Dixit, A. K. (1989), 'Hysterisis, import penetration and exchange rate pass-through', *Quarterly Journal of Economics*, Vol. 104, 225–8.

Dixit, A. K. and V. Norman (1980), *The Theory of International Trade: A Dual General Equilibrium Approach*, Cambridge: Nisbet.

Eichengreen, B. (1990), 'One money for Europe? Lessons from the US currency union', *Economic Policy*, April, 118–87.

El-Agraa, A. M. (1990), *The Economics of European Common Market*, 3rd edition, New York/London: Philip Allan.

Emerson, M., M. Aujean, M. Catinat, P. Goybet and A. Jacquemin (1988), *The Economics of 1992*, Oxford: Oxford University Press for the EC Commission.

Emerson, M., D. Gros and A. Alexander (1992), *One Market: One Money: An Evaluation of Potential Benefits and Costs of Forming an Economic and Monetary Union*, Oxford: Oxford University Press.

Ethier, W. (1988), *Modern International Economics*, 2nd edition, New York/London: W. W. Norton.

Feldstein, M. (1992), 'The case against European monetary union', *The Economist*, 13 June.

Flam, H. (1992), 'Product markets and 1992: Full integration, large gains?', *Journal of Economic Perspectives*, Vol. 6, 4, 7–30.

Frankel, J. A. (1991), 'Is a yen block forming in eastern Asia?', in Richard O'Brien, ed., *Finance and the International Economy 5*, Oxford: Oxford University Press for the American Express Bank.

Froot, K. A. and P. D. Klemperer (1988), 'Exchange rate pass-through when market share matters', *American Economic Review*, Vol. 79, 637–54.

Gagon, J. E. (1993), 'Exchange rate variability and the level of international trade', *Journal of International Economics*, Vol. 34, 269–87.

GATT (1986), *Text of the General Agreement on Tariffs and Trade*, Geneva: GATT.

Giavazzi, F. and A. Giovannini (1990), *Limiting Exchange Rate Flexibility: The European Monetary System*, Cambridge, Mass.: MIT Press.

Grossman, G. (1992), *Imperfect Competition and International Trade*, Cambridge, Mass.: MIT Press.

Helpman, E. and P. R. Krugman (1985), *Market Structure and Foreign Trade*, Cambridge, Mass.: MIT Press.

Helpman, E. and P. R. Krugman (1989), *Trade Policy and Market Structure*, Cambridge, Mass.: MIT Press.

Jackson, J. H. (1990), *Restructuring the GATT System*, London: Royal Institute of International Affairs/Pinter.

Johnson, H. G. (1965), 'An economic theory of protectionism, tariff bargaining and the formation of customs unions', *Journal of Political Economy*, Vol. 73, 256–83.

Jovanović, M. N. (1992), *International Economic Integration*, London: Routledge.

Kemp, M. C. and H. Y. Wan (1976), 'An elementary proposition concerning the formation of customs unions', *Journal of International Economics*, Vol. 6, 95–7.

Kenen, P. (1969), 'The theory of optimum currency areas: an eclectic view', in R. A. Mundell and A. K. Swoboda, eds, *Monetary Problems of the International Economies*, Chicago: Chicago University Press, 41–60.

Kierzkowski, H. (1987), 'Recent advances in international trade: a selective survey', *Oxford Review of Economic Policy*, Vol. 3, 1, 1–19.

Krueger, A. O. (1974), 'The political economy of the rent-seeking society', *American Economic Review*, Vol. 64, 291–303.

Krueger, A. O. (1984), 'Trade policies in developing countries', Ch. 11 in R. W. Jones and P. B. Kenen, eds, *Handbook of International Economics*, Amsterdam: North-Holland.

Krugman, P. R. (1984), 'Import protection as export promotion: international competition in the presence of oligopoly and economies of scale', in H. Kierzkowski, ed., *Monopolistic*

Competition and International Trade, Oxford: Clarendon Press.
Krugman, P. R., ed. (1986), *Strategic Trade Policy and the New International Economics*, Cambridge, Mass.: MIT Press.
Krugman, P. R. (1989), *Exchange Rate Instability*, Cambridge, Mass.: MIT Press.
Krugman, P. R. (1991a), 'Is bilateralism bad?', in E. Helpman and A. Razin, eds, *International Trade and Trade Policy*, Cambridge, Mass.: MIT Press.
Krugman, P. R. (1991b), *Geography and Trade*, Cambridge, Mass.: MIT Press.
Krugman, P. R. (1992), 'Does the new trade theory require a new trade policy?', *The World Economy*, Vol. 15, 4, 423–41.
Lawrence, R. Z. (1991), 'Emerging regional arrangements: building blocks or stumbling blocks?' in Richard O'Brien, ed., *Finance and the International Economy 5*, Oxford/London: Oxford University Press for the American Express Bank.
Magee, S. P. (1978), 'Three simple tests of the Stolper–Samuelson theorem', in P. Oppenheimer, ed., *Issues in International Economics*, Stocksfield, England: Oriel Press.
Magee, S. P., W. A. Brock and L. Young (1989), *Black Hole Tariffs and Endogenous Policy Theory: Political Economy in General Equilibrium*, Cambridge: Cambridge University Press.
Malinvaud, E. (1985), *Lectures on Microeconomic Theory*, Amsterdam: North-Holland.
Minford, P., ed. (1992), *The Cost of Europe*, Manchester: Manchester University Press.
Mundell, R. (1961), 'The theory of optimum currency areas', *American Economic Review*, September, 657–65.
Newbery, D. M. G. and J. E. Stiglitz (1981), *The Theory of Commodity Price Stabilization: A Study in the Economics of Risk*, Oxford: Clarendon Press.
Ohyama, M. (1972), 'Trade and welfare in general equilibrium', *Keio Economic Studies*, Vol. 9, 2, 37–73.
Robertson, D. (1992), 'GATT rules for emergency protection', *Thames Essays*, New York/London: Harvester Wheatsheaf for the Trade Policy Research Centre.
Rubinfield, D. L. (1987), 'The economics of the local public sector', in A. J. Auerbach and M. Feldstein, eds, *Handbook of Public Economics*, Vol. 2, Amsterdam: Elsevier.
Rudden B. and D. Wyatt (1993), *Basic Community Law*, 4th edition, Oxford: Clarendon Press.

Rybczynski, T. M. (1955), 'Factor endowments and relative commodity prices', *Economica*, Vol. 22, 336–41.

Shackleton, M. (1990), *Financing the European Community*, London: Royal Institute of International Affairs/Pinter.

Smith, Adam (1960), *The Wealth of Nations*, Everyman's Library, London: J. M. Dent & Son Ltd.

Smith, S. (1993), '"Subsidiarity" and the co-ordination of indirect taxes in the European community', *Oxford Review of Economic Policy*, Vol. 9, 1, 67–94.

Stiglitz, J. E. (1983), 'The theory of local public goods twenty-five years after Tiebout: A perspective', in J. F. Thisse and H. G. Zoller, eds, *Local Provision of Public Services: The Tiebout Model after Twenty-five Years*, New York: Academic Press, 17–54.

Stolper, W. F. and P. A. Samuelson (1941), 'Protection and real wages', *Review of Economic Studies*, Vol. 9, 58–73.

Tiebout, W. (1956), 'A pure theory of local government expenditures', *Journal of Political Economy*, Vol. 94, 416–24.

Tirole, J. (1988), *The Theory of Industrial Organization*, Cambridge, Mass.: MIT Press.

Varian, H. R. (1984), *Microeconomic Analysis*, 2nd edition, New York/London: W. W. Norton.

Walters, A. A. (1990), *Sterling in Danger: The Economic Consequences of Pegged Exchange Rates*, London: Fontana/Collins.

Williamson, J. (1983), *The Exchange Rate System*, Washington DC: Institute for International Economics.

Winters, L. A. (1990), 'The road to Uruguay', *Economic Journal*, Vol. 100, December, 1288–303.

Winters, L. A. (1991a), *International Economics*, 4th edition, London: HarperCollinsAcademic.

Winters, L. A. (1991b), 'Digging for victory', *The World Economy*, Vol. 13, 170–90.

Wonnacot, P. and R. Wonnacot (1981), 'Is unilateral tariff reduction preferable to a customs union? The curious case of the missing foreign tariffs', *American Economic Review*, Vol. 71, 704–14.

Yarrow, G. (1987), 'Economic aspects of anti-dumping policies', *Oxford Review of Economic Policy*, Vol. 3, 1, 66–79.

Index